Living Out Loud

A Daughter's Destiny

MARILYN TURNER

Anointed Fire™ House

Living Out Loud
A Daughter's Destiny
Copyright © 2016
Author:
Marilyn Turner
Email: mlltnhim@gmail.com

Publisher: Anointed Fire™ House
Publisher's Website: www.anointedfirehouse.com

<u>**All scriptures noted in this book were taken from the King James Bible, American King James Version, New Living Testament or Amplified Bible unless otherwise noted.**</u>

ISBN-13: 978-0692674475

ISBN-10: 0692674470

DEDICATION

This book is Dedicated

In Loving Memory of

Cynthia Marcella Martino

October 28, 2015

Table of Contents

Acknowledgments

There are so many reasons to be thankful and a few people I'd like to thank.

First and foremost, I have to shout "Thank you, Father, Jesus, the Son and the Holy Ghost for making yourself REAL to me! For giving me freedom and a fresh start with purpose and destiny so that I can 'live out loud' for You!"

To my parents, Willard and Marcia Love and all my family (the Loves, Bates and Richbows): Thank you.

To my siblings (Stephanie, Pepper, Willard Jr., Scotty, Robin, Davina) and to all the cousins we grew up with... you know who you are: In regards to our childhood, as Charles Dickens wrote, "It was the best of times, it was the worst of times..." Nevertheless, we all made it out. My prayer for you is that somehow this book inspires you to make more "best times" than "worst times" for the rest of your lives in Christ. You didn't choose me to be your sibling or family member, but thank you for the fond memories and for loving me just the same.

I want to say thank you to the circle of friends and mentorship God gave me in my early Christian walk. There are three women in particular.

The late, Cyndi Martino, my first sister in Christ, who God used to draw me back to Him.

To Annzella Victoria Watkins, my first mentor: You told me the truth, prayed with me, and inspired me to read my Bible. I'm so grateful for our continued friendship.

To Taji Coleman, my sister and friend in Christ who set a fine example of being a Christian actress in Hollywood: Thank you for keeping it holy.

I would be remiss if I didn't' acknowledge a few women who God used to help birth this book; for them, I am forever grateful.

First, Pastor Shanda Lyons, who after having heard my testimony, planted the seed for this book.

My "midwife," editor and publisher, Tiffany Buckner: Thank you for your expertise, wisdom, and motivation.

Thank you to Janelle Mitchell for lending your ear to listen as I read out loud each chapter of this book. Your time and kind words have been a huge blessing.

To my dear assistant, Martine Banossian, who helps me keep it all together: No matter what, you are always there to rise to any occasion. Thank you for your time, resources, and support. My affection for you runs deep.

Thank you to the New Hope International Ministries Church family. I love you all! You all are so dear to me. I count it a reward to be able to meet with you on a weekly basis, encouraging you on your spiritual journey with Christ. I pray that this book inspires you to live 100% Out Loud for Christ.

Lastly, and certainly not least, to my husband, Apostle Charles Turner III, my happily ever after and my best friend: Thank for choosing me as your wife. Certainly, you are my number one inspiration for "Living Out Loud!" You set the example for no compromise, keeping it 100% real. Thank you for your conviction to hold me to the gifts, talents, and abilities God has given me. You remind me daily that I am treasured, loved and full of purpose and destiny. Oh, how I love you, man of God! I'm forever grateful for you.

Foreword

This wonderful book is an enthusiastic celebration of life and many victories in Christ, especially those victories that are of deliverance origin. The author is transparent as she shares details of her own intricate life, and she allows us to walk alongside her as she shares her personal journey of an intimate relationship with Christ. She emphasizes the need for a real commitment to discipleship and healing from our pasts in order to become true overcomers.

Her personal testimony is a unique tribute to the many women who have experienced any sort of crisis, rejection or disappointment in their lives. Although the emphasis of this work is about a unique life struggle, it contains much that will be of interest to those with a sincere desire to overcome the world's heartbreaks through the healing power of Jesus.

The author has chosen to open her life about real candid key issues such as addiction, abortion, and depression. It's a wonderful inspirational story of how she pressed through difficult controversial circumstances to become the woman she is today. She provides a roadmap on how she rose from ashes to beauty and became the Author, Playwright, Actress, Minister, First Lady and Wife she is today. This book amplifies the power of faith and determination through the journey of a Christ-driven life.

I think any reader who delves into this book will have gained a broader perspective of the discipline it takes to achieve success. In spite of the roadblocks that life can present when you add faith in Christ, as this author has pointed out, you can achieve your destiny. All it takes is faith, grace, effort and determination. God bless you, Prophetess Marilyn Turner for sharing your life with the world.

Apostle Charles Turner III
NHIM Worship Center, Florida

Living Out Loud

A Daughter's Destiny

Chapter One

The Turning Point: My Truth: Deliverance

"And it came to pass afterward, that he went throughout every city and village, preaching and shewing the glad tidings of the kingdom of God: and the twelve were with him, And certain women, which had been healed of evil spirits and infirmities, Mary called Magdalene, out of whom went seven devils..."
Luke 8:1-3

There was a time when I was going through something in my life. It was so devastating that I thought I would not be able to make it through without caving back into my past weaknesses. All I knew to do at the time was to muster up all of my strength and cry out to God. At the time, I didn't have a close relationship with Jesus, but I did know that He is the Savior of the world and the one God the Father sent to give us eternal life. Only a few years prior did I have my "come to Jesus moment." At that time, I joined a local church and went part way through new members' class, but unfortunately, the cares of life caused me to go back into the world. So, while I was going through, all I really knew to do was to cry out to God. I loved God, even though I was not serving Him the way He deserved.

For a space of about three weeks, I would pace up and down my house in California day and night saying to myself and to God... "I'm not going back there... I will make it through this hard time... I will not go back to that place... whatever it takes, I'm not going back to where I have come from!" Only I and God knew what "that place" was. In my mind, I could see myself with my crutches in my hand, a bottle of vodka and a straw for snorting my false security: cocaine. I could see myself falling back into darkness, "that place" that God had supernaturally delivered me from only a few years prior. At this point in my life, I had a few years of sobriety under my belt; however, I was living a life of victory over the power of those addictions... or so I thought. Unbeknownst to me, my mindset was still bound by my old lifestyle and needed to be renewed. Also, there were dark forces at work in me that were opposing the will of God. I had great battles of depression coupled with emotional dilemmas...all of which caused my life to come to a screeching halt.

What I was going through at the time was God's plan for my life. Contrary to how it looked, He was intervening in my life in a wonderful way. You see, during this season in my life, I was in Hollywood pursuing an acting career. At this point, I had done print work, television commercials, a sitcom and several stage plays with famous people. I thought that with a little hard work, faith and perseverance, I was on my way to a breakthrough in my career. I would be able to live out my dreams of becoming a working actress in Hollywood, making a good living doing what I had been born to do. In fact, I had just finished two stage plays back to back and they'd received great reviews, one of which received a prestigious award. Next for me, was a leading role in an independent film. This was my big break and I was up to the challenge. I even cut my long dark hair off for the role (it was something I had wanted to do for a while anyway). So here I was getting ready to embark on another level in my career. It was a wonderful challenge and opportunity.

The first day on the set was difficult and it ended with disappointment. The director was very patient and confident that things would go better on the next day, but the next day proved to be worse. Still, the director encouraged me, and he was confident that I would get it together by the next day. The third day was a disaster and it ended with me sobbing on the shoulders of my consoling director. It was very humiliating. In those first few days of shooting, I was experiencing something I couldn't understand. I was closed up and shut down. I couldn't let anything in and couldn't let anything out creatively. It was as if I knew nothing at all about acting.

I had just finished a play in which I was hired to replace a cast member only ten days before opening night. I had my lines, stage direction and character ready for that first night and we received great reviews. The director of this film had seen my previous work and was convinced that I was the character I was hired to portray and had what it took to bring her to life. However, what he did next had to be a God-thing. He shut down production, hired an acting coach, and for a period of two weeks, I worked with her. From day one, she couldn't understand why I needed her, nevertheless, we continued meeting. When the director inquired, she assured him that it was safe to begin production again; she assured him that I was more than ready.

Back on the set, day one proved to be another disastrous day. The same symptoms were there. Day two was even worse. At that point, the director decided to shut down again and made a decision to begin to look for another actress with the stipulation that in one week, he would meet with me for one last chance. Clearly, God was not ready to release me from my trial.

Apart from humiliation, I felt like my dream was being ripped away from me yet again. I was crushed. Even though I couldn't understand how and why this was happening to me, a part of me was convinced that it was just my lot since I had experienced many disappointments in my life. This was just another one. In the back of my mind, I heard a voice telling me that dreams do come true for people... just not for me. This voice had me convinced that I was unworthy and did not deserve to see my dreams come to pass. Nevertheless, I could not let go; there was still a fight in me. I continued to cry out to God for help.

During this time, I began to pay attention to this quiet, small voice that I was not acquainted with. I know now that it was the Holy Spirit. This voice had been telling me for the past few weeks to call my friend Cyndi. Cyndi was someone who I had befriended about one or two years earlier during a play that we were in together. We became great friends after her car blew its engine. While she was in the process of shopping for a new one, she rode with me to our play rehearsals and shows, since we lived near each other. I looked forward to those days because even though I wasn't a church-going person, I loved to hear her talk about God and tell me the awesome things He had done for her since we were last together. I loved to hear a good testimony and she was full of them. To this day, she is one of my best friends and favorite people.

Finally, I paid attention to that gentle voice and reached out to my friend. I explained the situation to her. While on the phone, Cyndi kept saying little things that didn't make sense to me. It was as if she were talking to someone other than me. Though I thought it was strange, I just chalked it off. I would come to understand later that she was having a conversation with the Holy Spirit. He was giving her instructions on what to do. Reflecting on this reminds me just how much God loves me. It's amazing that He would give another person wisdom on how to help me. She reassured me that everything would be okay and then asked if she could drop by to see me that afternoon.

True to her word, she arrived as promised and I began to give her a deeper explanation as to what was going on. Afterwards, she said some good Christian words, let me know she believed in my ability as an actress and reassured me that she would help me win this role. What happened next was the reason God sent Cyndi to me.

She asked if she could pray for me before leaving. I said yes. As we sat side by side on the couch in my living room, we locked hands and she began to talk to God for me. Within a few minutes into the prayer, she switched from making a prayer to God to talking to me. She began by saying, "Marilyn, God says that He doesn't want you to go back to 'that place' either." At that moment, that same picture of me with the vodka and straw for cocaine came back to mind. I remembered that that was what I had been talking to God about and she had not been privy to that information, yet she used the exact words I had spoken to God. Needless to say, God had my attention.

I had never experienced anything like that before, but I knew God was talking to me through my friend, Cyndi. I later learned that the Holy Spirit was working with her prophetically in a word of knowledge and wisdom. He continued to show her things she could not have known. She went on to say, "Marilyn, God says that you give Him glory for everything good that happens in your life." "Yes, I do," I responded. That was true; it was my habit to write letters to Him about everything that was going on in my life, and when something good happened, not only would I write a letter of thanks, I wasn't shy to brag about Him to others. Then she said "But when something bad happens to you..." We both finished the sentence together, only she said it audibly; I said it within my heart, "You blame yourself." I answered God out loud this time by saying, "Yes, I do." At that moment, I received a revelation about myself and my spiritual condition. I had never looked at it in this light before, but the truth was that I blamed myself for an awful lot. I was pretty hard on myself. I could not deny this.

She then told me that God said I had to forgive myself. God is so amazing; the manner in which He caused me to arrive at this revelation made me see that indeed, there was a need to forgive myself. There was no way around that fact. The problem was that even though I recognized this need, I had no idea how to forgive myself. So within my heart, I told God, "I know I need to. I'm willing, but I just don't know how." Just as I finished my thought, without warning, there came a sharp tug on my body and it caused me to simultaneously stiffen up from my head to my arms and down through my shoulders to my waist. Though I had my eyes closed, I think at that point, Cyndi may have been a little alarmed because for a second, I could tell her eyes were wide open. What happened next came from the deepest crevice of my loins, from far down in the very deepest place in me. Out came a guttural roar that got louder and more intense as it reached my mouth and it came out loudly. My body began to rock back and forth by a force from within me. I could feel Cyndi take a strong grip on both of my hands as I continued to shake and let out one guttural scream after another. All the while, I could feel something tearing away from within me. It was as if God had reached His hand through my mouth and down to the deepest part of me, wrapped His hand around something to get a good grip, and then slowly began to pull the root of it upward and out. It was a dichotomy, where this ugly and dirty feeling was leaving my body; at the same time, something beautiful, warm and loving was overwhelming me. The best way to describe it is... it was as if a huge dark presence was being lifted up and out of me. I felt like at last, a large, beautiful flower was finally able to bloom inside of me. On one hand, I felt the most uncomfortable feeling I had ever felt, and at the same time, the most comforting feeling I had ever felt. All of a sudden, it was over.

Cyndi took me into her bosom and began to explain to me what had just happened. I had just been delivered from indwelling demons. She told me that she had seen three demons leave my body and they were the spirits of shame, unworthiness, and rejection. She also told me that if they tried to come back, I was to reject them by telling them that they are not welcome. I was also noticing the strong sense of God's love and peace; this feeling had overtaken all of my senses.

After a few moments, I asked Cyndi if I could go to church with her. Ordinarily, church would have been the furthest thing from my mind since I had endured a bad experience in a church the previous year. At that point, I had known Cyndi for a few years and the Holy Spirit knew that if Cyndi had invited me to go to church with her before this experience, I would have avoided her like the plague. Instead, there I was asking her. It just came out of my mouth and I found myself sincerely agreeing with that request. Cyndi answered, and amazingly enough, it just so happened that she would be going to Bible study in just a few short hours. It's wonderful how God set my deliverance day to be the very day of the week that Cyndi went to Bible study.

That evening at Bible study, I wrote my first tithe check, became a regular church attendee and a worshipper. I have not looked back since. I call this experience my "turning point." I was a new woman. I was like Mary of Magdala, out of whom seven demons came out. After her deliverance, she followed Jesus.

Did I get to make that film? About a week later, I met with the director and he had an opportunity to work with a big name actress, so he took it. Was I disappointed? Nope. Somehow, I knew God never meant for me to make that film; He just used it to bring me to my "turning point", and I'm ever so grateful. I know I had received the better portion.

Chapter Two

<u>Forgiveness of Self: Freedom</u>

"Then the angry king sent the man to prison to be tortured until he had paid his entire debt. That's what my heavenly Father will do to you if you refuse to forgive your brothers and sisters from your heart."
Matthew 18:34-35 NLT

Right before getting delivered of three demons: the spirits of shame, unworthiness and rejection, God used my friend, Cyndi, to lead me in a prayer of repentance to forgive myself. This prayer was very necessary if I was going to be released from those demons. I was my own worst enemy. I was holding myself hostage and holding a debt over my own head that I could never repay. In effect, I was being tortured because of unforgiveness. The thing about it is that I had no idea that I had unforgiveness in my heart towards myself; the thought had never even occurred to me. Looking back, I suppose had I paid closer attention to my thought life and actions, I may have been able to figure it out on my own. I just thank God for His tender mercies toward me, doing for me what I could not do for myself.

In the prayer, God first got my attention. He fixed my spiritual eyes back on Him. He was letting me know that He heard the cry of my heart, He was compassionate towards my pain and most importantly, He reminded me that He was the same God who forgave me for my past wrongdoing.

Just a few years earlier, I was invited to church by a dear friend who was like a family member. She had been praying for me. She was privy to my lifestyle of drinking, drugging and staying out in the clubs until all hours of the night. I don't believe that she ever judged me. I think she saw that I was miserable and in a dangerous emotional state. She knew that what I needed in order to be free, only Jesus could give. That's someone who cares.

I wasn't the kind of drinker who just had a few drinks for happy hour. If I had one drink, I would continue to drink until I passed out or when the alcohol ran out. There were plenty of nights when I functioned in a "black out" state and woke up the next morning or afternoon wondering what happened the night before. Drugs, for me, were the same way and cocaine happened to be my drug of choice. I was so addicted to cocaine that if I simply thought about it, a strong craving for it would overcome me and all I could think to do was to go out and give in to that desire. I was in a miserable state. I was tormented.

I had become a slave to drugs, alcohol, my own flesh, and the devil (the ultimate enemy of my soul). Romans 6:16 NLT states, "Don't you realize that you become the slave of whatever you choose to obey? You can be a slave to sin, which leads to death, or you can choose to obey God, which leads to righteous living." I was smoking cigarettes, drinking alcohol, and eventually, I started using cocaine. No one could tell me that there was something wrong with my lifestyle. At first, I did these things casually, whenever a group of us friends got together on weekends. In truth, I was rebelling against God. After awhile, "casually" became "habitually." I wasn't aware of this at the time, but the first time I indulged in these things, I yielded my power over to drugs, alcohol, cigarettes, my own will and the devil. The longer I continued on this road of destruction, the deeper the passion and addiction. At this point in my life, my mind was so depraved; I was the epitome of Philippians 3:19 NIV, "They are headed for destruction. Their destiny is destruction, their god is their stomach, and their glory is in their shame. Their mind is set on earthly things." I was so enslaved that at the end of my addiction, I was drinking straight vodka out of a bottle and I had become somewhat of a recluse, sitting at home and trying to get high on cocaine. Ironically enough, the cocaine didn't do it for me anymore. I couldn't get high on it. Eventually, I tried to end my own life. Even when I wanted the merry-go-round to stop, I found that I had no power within myself to stop it. I bless God for saving me!

On that Sunday, my friend came to get me for church bright and early. I didn't realize it at the time, but this would be the day that I would enter a season of change. Back then, I had no idea someone could be touched by the preaching of the gospel. The Bible does state that the Word of God is quick and powerful, sharper than a double edge sword (see Hebrews 4:12). The Word of God cut through my soul so deep on that morning, I thought the preacher had been spying on me beforehand to get a message. Whatever the case, I heard him loud and clear.

For the first time in my life, I clearly heard the message of the gospel. I could see from the fruit of my depraved lifestyle that I was a sinner. Even though God loved me with an everlasting love, I was separated from Him because of my sinful and rebellious choices in life. I came to the realization that God didn't want me to suffer the way I was suffering and this is why He sent His only begotten Son into the world to die on the cross. It was because He loved me that He sent His Son as a scapegoat so that my sins could be forgiven, which allowed me to come into fellowship with the Father and receive eternal life. If I could just believe this, be willing to confess that I was a sinner and ask for forgiveness, I would be forgiven.

This was significant to me because I felt like I was the worst of sinners. I had done so much wrong in my life and had messed up so badly that there seemed to be no hope for me. From drugs and alcohol to the people I had been associating myself with, the promiscuous behavior, the abortions I had, and the many other wrongs that came with my lifestyle, I thought I was a lost cause. I was guilty. No one has to tell a sinner they are guilty; they are told this by their own conscience. What I needed to be told was that there was a solution.

On that morning, I saw Jesus, the suffering Savior as the solution to my sufferings. As the preacher ministered the altar call, I didn't hesitate to come down to receive this

Savior into my heart; my friend walked with me to the altar. With sobbing and tears, I repeated the sinners' prayer sincerely in my heart and received Christ. I had been forgiven. As the scripture tells us, God had removed my sins as far from me as the east is from the west (see Psalm 103:12 NLT). My sins were blotted out. I felt like a new woman with a new lease on life just as the Bible promises us in 2 Corinthians 5:17, "Therefore if any man be in Christ, he is a new creature: old things are passed away; behold, all things are become new." Because I simply asked to be forgiven, God forgave me. Every wrong that I had done had been forgotten in His eyes. The slate was wiped clean and I was free. I was officially in a new season of my life! Not long after, through a succession of events, I was free from drugs, alcohol and the sinful lifestyle I had been leading. I started attending church on a regular basis and everything looked like it was on the up for me.

However, after awhile, though I never went back to cocaine and alcohol, I began to backslide in church attendance. After experiencing several crises in my life, I had even begun to smoke again. I still loved God and had a conviction to have a relationship with Him, but I attempted to have that relationship on my terms. Eventually, my spiritual momentum came to a standstill.

I now understand two significant things. First, God forgave me of all the atrocities of my old lifestyle and I had received

His forgiveness, but I had never forgiven myself of all these atrocities. Because of this, there was a spiritual principle at work in my life that caused emotional hardship. Next, I didn't understand that God uses hardship, affliction and trials in our lives to shape and mold our character and strengthen our faith. Instead of looking at all the bad in my life and taking the blame, I needed to praise God for it because it was an opportunity to grow and know Him more. Like Job said when he was going through his afflictions, "Shall we indeed accept good from God, and shall we not accept adversity?" (see Job 2:10 NKJV). I was taking credit for something that God was doing. He was working out all things for my good. I couldn't see it because I had a habit of blaming myself.

God's wisdom is infinite. He knew just how to get me to the place of seeing for myself that I had unforgiveness in my heart. I had to admit it in order to be forgiven. This is why I say that God led me to a prayer of repentance for the sin of unforgiveness. In order to get to the place of admission, I first needed a revelation of my sin. Repentance is about having your eyes opened to what sin is so that you have a changing of the mind about what sin is. In Acts 26:18, the apostle Paul said this was his commission from Jesus to the Gentiles, "To open their eyes, and to turn them from darkness to light, and from the power of Satan unto God, that they may receive forgiveness of sins, and inheritance among them which are sanctified by faith that is in me."

What's needed is a revelation of the wrongdoing so that there could be a turning away from it. How did God do that for me? He showed me first how I gave Him credit for only the good that was happening in my life. Then He pointed out my sin; He showed me that I was putting blame on myself for all the bad. In fact, I was judging and condemning myself. Even though I was not aware of this sin, God could not release me from the power of darkness and Satan because I kept committing it over and over. I was truly in prison. Jesus said in Matthew, the sixth chapter, as He taught us to pray, "And forgive us our debts, as we forgive our debtors" (Matthew 6:12). He went on to say in verses 14 and 15 of that same chapter, "For if ye forgive men their trespasses, your heavenly Father will also forgive you. But if ye forgive not men their trespasses, neither will your Father forgive your trespasses." In Matthew 18:23-35, Jesus taught the same principle in the parable of the unforgiving servant. He taught that our trespasses are debts owed to God, but because we had no way of paying them back to Him, He simply forgave us. Likewise, we are to do the same for others.

This principle applies to the unforgiveness of self. I was not exempt from God's law, and even though He loved me, unless I confessed this sin, I could not be forgiven. In the parable of the unforgiving servant, because of his unwillingness to forgive, he was handed over to the tormentors until he paid all. The sad thing about this is that because he was sent to prison to be tortured, he had no opportunity of ever paying it back. Much like myself, even though the people around me couldn't see it, I was being tormented by Satan because of the unforgiveness in my heart. I was depressed, discouraged all the time and an emotional mess. My mind was full of negative thoughts. Satan had a well- built playground in my head and he came out to play often... rain or shine. When God opened my eyes to this sin, I needed to confess it. I John 1:9 shows us something about our merciful God that we need to be aware of and it reads, "If we confess our sins, he is faithful and just to forgive us our sins, and to cleanse us from all unrighteousness." Biblical confession is about saying the same thing about sin that God says about sin. I had to confess that I blamed myself because God said that this is sin. As I made my confession, I became one step away from being delivered from the power of darkness.

In that moment, I could see so clearly that forgiveness of self was needed. I just couldn't wrap my mind around the concept of actually doing it. I didn't have a clue. Interestingly, it was quite easy for me to forgive others. I was able to show mercy to those who trespassed against me, but when it came to me, that was a different story. This was a new concept to me. I now know that to some degree, it had to do with low self-esteem and low self-worth due to the indwelling personalities of unworthiness, shame, and rejection. Because I had been rejected by others, I rejected myself. I thought something was wrong with me. Because shameful events happened in my life, I was ashamed, and shame lingered with me; this caused me to feel guilty. There had been times when I was treated as if I was worthless by others, so I thought I was unworthy of any good thing, including love. These events opened the door for those spirits to come in and oppress me in order to express themselves through me. So, at that moment in prayer with Cyndi, as I recognized the need, I wrestled with how I was to go about forgiving myself. I was wrapped up in emotions and intellect that were related to self-rejection and unworthiness, not love.

In my ministry today, I come across people who struggle with a lack of self-forgiveness as I did. Sometimes, we are harder on ourselves than we are with others who have mishandled and offended us. In such cases, we must remember that forgiveness is not based on our feelings or intellect. It's not based on whether we feel we deserve it. Forgiving others is a decision we make based on God's commandment to forgive. We must forgive ourselves in the same manner that we forgive others. When we forgive others, it is out of our mercy, compassion, love, and most importantly, our willingness to be obedient to God's command. He said if we do not forgive others, we will not be forgiven (see Matthew

6:15). We simply make the decision to forgive and become willing to put that forgiveness in motion. He set the example for us; look at what Jeremiah 33:8 NIV records, "I will cleanse them from all the sin they have committed against me and will forgive all their sins of rebellion against me." He said, "I will cleanse" and "will forgive." His willingness is a testimony to His deciding to forgive us. He made a willful decision to provide a way for sinful man to be forgiven because He loves us. God loved us so much He decided to do something about our fallen state, and then He sent His Son, Jesus, as the Lamb of God, who covers our sins.

We must forgive as God forgave. He was willing to forgive us because He loved us. We have been freely given that love. Romans 5:5 teaches us that God lavishly poured His love upon our hearts by placing the Holy Spirit in us. When we tap into that love in our hearts, it helps us to become willing to forgive, but it is our simple decision to forgive that God honors. In that moment and in that prayer, God was there. God is love. I was intoxicated with His love, so much so that I had become aware of my sin of unforgiveness and had become willing to forgive myself. It didn't matter if I didn't know how to forgive myself. God just needed my will to be turned over to Him. Much like Jesus, who before going to the cross said to the Father, "Father, if it is Your will, take this cup away from Me; nevertheless not My will, but Yours, be done" (Luke 22:42 NKJV). When I said "I'm willing," that was all God needed.

I'm a living testimony of the grace of God. My WILLINGNESS to forgive myself was all God needed; it had little to do with how I was 'feeling' at the time. Because I chose to forgive, regardless of whether I knew how to, He did the rest! In 2 Corinthians 12:9, the great apostle Paul asked the Lord to remove a thorn from his flesh because a messenger of Satan would periodically come and take advantage of that weakness. This is how the Lord responded, "And he said unto me, My grace is sufficient for thee: for my strength is made perfect in weakness." Notice, the Lord said His grace was all that was needed, and then He referred to His grace as "strength" made perfect in weakness. It's when we recognize and acknowledge our weaknesses to the Lord that He helps us to do what we can't do. When I said to God that I was willing but didn't know how to forgive myself, I was admitting to Him that I was weak in the area of forgiveness. His grace kicked in and delivered me from the power of darkness and from Satan. God put supernatural strength into my willingness.

In that same passage, Paul went on to say, "Most gladly therefore will I rather glory in my infirmities, that the power of Christ may rest upon me." I'm a testimony to the power of Christ resting upon me for deliverance. I was released out of the prison of shame and depression. Those demons of shame, unworthiness, and rejection no longer had permission to stay in me. That unassuming afternoon on my living room couch was the day I saw God's grace, not just as unmerited favor to me, but I saw it in action. I saw the power of His grace and His willingness to set me free. My deliverance was proof that when I repented, confessed and acknowledged my sins and weaknesses, God accepted my repentance. I was finally free!

Not long after my deliverance, God began to address my emotions, regrets, the consequences of wrong decisions and having been oppressed by indwelling demons. I now needed to learn how to keep the past in the past and not look back. I didn't know at the time that there was a great work God was calling me to. I had to be whole, and not just in the context of having the promise of eternal life when I leave this earth, but He wanted me whole: soul, spirit, and body.

Paul said, "This one thing I do, forgetting those things which are behind, and reaching forth unto those things which are before..." (Philippians 3:13). Paul was a murderer who killed Christians before his encounter with Jesus on the road to Damascus. If he was not willing to forgive himself for this, he would not have been able to do the beautiful work he was called to do for God in serving the church. In my present life, when I look back to my past, it is only to give God glory and to tell others about the powerful grace of God.

Chapter Three

<u>At the Feet of Jesus: Worship</u>

"And, behold, a woman in the city, which was a sinner, when she knew that Jesus sat at meat in the Pharisee's house, brought an alabaster box of ointment, And stood at his feet behind him weeping, and began to wash his feet with tears, and did wipe them with the hairs of her head, and kissed his feet, and anointed them with the ointment."
Luke 7:37-38

B efore my deliverance, I was that woman at the well in John 4:7-26, whose lifestyle caused her to feel ashamed, rejected, and condemned. She was a broken woman who chose to walk to the well for water at the hottest point of the day just to avoid the ridicule of the townspeople. On this day, the woman encountered Jesus at the well and He told her, "Whosoever drinketh of this water shall thirst again: But whosoever drinketh of the water that I shall give him shall never thirst; but the water that I shall give him shall be in him a well of water springing up into everlasting life" (John 4:13-14).

In this story, Jesus pointed out that she was looking to fill a spiritual void with natural things. He referenced the fact that she had had five husbands and was presently working on a sixth. In other words, she was going about her natural life all wrong, with one dynamic missing: true worship. Because of this, she would never be fulfilled. Something was wrong in her life. Like this woman, I was also looking to quench a spiritual thirst with the natural things of the world. This "natural water" was like a shallow refreshing coming to me from without, only lasting a moment and would soon have to be replenished as if I had never indulged.

At this time in my life, I had pretty much tried a little of everything and was still searching to get to a place of satisfaction. A few years earlier, I had received forgiveness for my sins and had been born again. I had been freed from the grip of alcohol, drugs, and the lifestyle and was convinced that none of those things were the answer. Unfortunately for me, before becoming rooted and grounded in the faith, and acquainted with the power and love of God in an intimate way, I went back into the world; I went back to living on my terms. I was headed down the same road I was on before being born again.

If someone had asked me if I was a Christian, I would have emphatically answered, "yes," and I was! I was a carnal Christian who didn't have a clue as to who God the Father, God the Son and God the Holy Spirit were and what was expected of me. Looking at my lifestyle just before deliverance from those evil spirits, one would not have known I loved God. Granted, I didn't have five or six husbands like the woman at the well, however, I was going through "boyfriends" as quick as a machine gun could fire bullets (if one could call them that). I was looking to my acting jobs to fulfill me, my wardrobe, and my earnings for the year to make me feel better. I also defined my worth by the parties I would be invited to, what circle of friends I had and the list goes on. I was searching for satisfaction in all the wrong places, but at the end of the day, I was still empty, lonely, and afraid. At the time, like the woman at the well, I didn't know Jesus was my all sufficiency.

In spite of the life I was living, I still had a burning desire to serve and worship God, but because I was living life on my terms, my worship was on my terms. I would pray whenever I had a financial need or when things weren't going right for me. I would sit and write letters to God most nights and even on my days off, and like God said during that prayer of deliverance, I gave Him credit for all the good in my life. Looking back, those letters were about what God could do for me or give to me. I poured out my heart to God almost on a daily basis; seldom did I listen for His response, ask to know Him or attempt to hear His voice. However, I must say, in the few times that I did ask to hear His voice or to know Him, I was sincere. I wanted to worship Him; I was just going about it wrong... in my own effort.

The woman at the well also had a curiosity on how to worship God. Perceiving only that Jesus was a prophet and not understanding yet that He was the Messiah, she seized the opportunity to ask Him about the common debate of that day. Who is right, my ancestors who say that the proper place to worship God is at this mountain or the Jews who say the proper place is Jerusalem? If you read the verses, you will see that Jesus confirmed the Jews were correct and that the Samaritans didn't completely understand what worship was. He went on to say that salvation was only available to the Jews. However, there was coming a time when salvation would be offered to all and worship would be practiced, not in an external way or at a physical place such as a mountain or city. Instead, there was coming a time when 'true worship' would come from an internal place. Notice, Jesus was talking about worship, but He mentions salvation, thus, signifying that our salvation is vital to our worship of God. Without it, we cannot truly worship Him. He explains, "But the hour is coming, and now is, when the true worshipers will worship the Father in spirit and truth; for the Father is seeking such to worship Him. God is Spirit, and those who worship Him must worship in spirit and truth" (John 4:23-24 NLT). We can learn from what Jesus said. God is looking for "true worshippers" and that "true worshippers" are those who worship, not by doing external homage, but from within the heart. This is why He mentioned that true worship came in truth; it came from a real relationship and experience of Him. He's describing a close fellowship relationship.

Upon our salvation experience, the Spirit of the living God comes into our spirits, our innermost beings, and makes His abode. Until we have this experience, we are separated from God, thereby, making it impossible to be a true worshipper. Romans 8:15-16 (NLT) confirms this, "So you have not received a spirit that makes you fearful slaves. Instead, you received God's Spirit when he adopted you as his own children. Now we call him, 'Abba, Father.' For his Spirit joins with our spirit to affirm that we are God's children."

Earlier, Jesus told the woman at the well that the water that He would give her would be within a fountain of water springing up into everlasting life. Jesus was showing Himself as the Messiah, the one who would, through His suffering on the cross, make worship from within possible. He later confirms this, "The woman said to Him, "I know that Messiah is coming (who is called Christ). When He comes, He will tell us all things." Jesus said to her, "I who speak to you am He" (John 4:25-26 NLT). This woman had a true encounter with the Messiah and because she believed, she was set free! She no longer had condemnation, shame or fear as she ran off boldly to tell the townspeople that the Messiah was there. The scriptures record that she left her watering pot, thus signifying that she no longer had a thirst for that "natural water." That meeting at the well with Jesus was satisfying enough, even in the heat of the day.

On the day of my deliverance, I was that woman at the well. My couch was the well and Jesus showed up. From that encounter, I can honestly say that there has been a fountain of living water flowing out of me, which has not ceased to this day. Certainly, I was ready to become a "true worshipper in spirit and in truth." Little did I know that I was about to embark on a journey that would change my life forever.

Thinking back to that moment on my journey, I now realize that I had experienced the Holy Spirit prior to that, but I just was unable to recognize Him. For example, I would sense His presence on those days when I would go out to sit in the park and write in my journal. Also, I heard His voice tell me to call my friend Cyndi and there were plenty of times when "something" told me what to do. Since the time of my new birth experience, He was there with me. Jesus promised this in Matthew 28:20, "And behold, I am with you always, to the end of the age." God also said, "I will never leave you nor forsake you" (Deuteronomy 31:6). The Holy Spirit in me was with me, but grieved because I was not living for Him. A better way of putting it is: I was not allowing Him to live through me.

As I was being delivered from the evil spirits on that day, the bands of wickedness, yokes of the enemy and the chains of oppression were removed from my spirit, causing me to feel alive again. At the same time, I received a fresh infilling of the Holy Spirit whose presence had filled my house earlier. Hence, I could experience His love reviving on the inside of me in an even more tangible way.

It's difficult to describe, but this was the fountain of water Jesus spoke of flowing on the inside of me. This love compelled me to want to get to know this Jesus, who I had fallen in love with all over again; only this time, much deeper. In a moment's time, I had a newfound hope for life. Somehow, I knew everything was going to be okay, and not just presently. Instead, a change had come on the inside of me and it changed me permanently. At that point, none of my circumstances had changed, yet I had a peace beyond my own understanding. It was as if Jesus had come on the scene and caused all of the storms within me to immediately be calm by simply saying, "Peace be still."

Even at Bible study that night, I rededicated my life to Jesus. I could hear the message of the gospel and it excited me all over again. I had such a hunger for God and a thirst for His Word. My soul wanted to know everything I could about this Jesus who delivered me from the tormentors. I was like Mary, Martha's sister, who sat at the feet of Jesus with her eyes fixed on Him, listening to every word that came out of His mouth. I wanted the better portion, that part that could not be taken away (see Luke 10:39-42).

I quickly learned that it was vitally important to start filling myself and my life with God. Otherwise, the demons would return and I would eventually find myself in the same situation or worse. Jesus taught this principle in Matthew 12:43-45, which reads, "When the unclean spirit is gone out of a man, he walketh through dry places, seeking rest, and findeth none. Then he saith, I will return into my house from whence I came out; and when he is come, he findeth it empty, swept, and garnished. Then goeth he, and taketh with himself seven other spirits more wicked than himself, and they enter in and dwell there: and the last state of that man is worse than the first..."

What is important to learn from this passage is that after an unclean spirit is cast out, it looks for rest but finds none. It will go back to its former house, and if that house is empty, it will return to it, bringing seven more wicked spirits with it that are more evil than itself. Take it from me, there's something about being delivered from evil spirits that makes you want to never travel down that road again.

Mary of Magdala, out of whom went seven devils, understood this principle all too well. She wanted to be where Jesus was. After having been "emptied" from seven demons, we can see her in the scriptures as an example of what it is to become a "true worshipper" of God. She began to fill her life with the presence of Jesus. Nowhere in the gospels do we read that she needed to be delivered again. There are, however, several accounts in the Bible that suggest she left her old lifestyle behind to follow Jesus. We can learn much about worship when we look at these accounts of her lifestyle after encountering Jesus.

First, we learn from Luke 8:1-3 that she was among the women named who followed Jesus and ministered to Him out of their substance. Jesus, in His earthly ministry, traveled the holy lands, preaching and teaching the gospel. If the Bible teaches us that she followed Christ and gave of her substance, it's safe to say then that she attended His church services, tithed and gave offerings to the work of His ministry on a regular basis. Secondly, she wasn't just a follower of Christ, but a faithful follower of Christ. John 19:25 tells us that she was at the cross when He finished His work; she was faithful till the end. Thirdly, John 20:1 reads, "The first day of the week cometh Mary Magdalene early, when it was yet dark..." She was willing to rise early in the morning in order to worship Jesus at the tomb where His body was laid. Next, her commitment to follow Jesus and worship Him birthed her ministry because, according to Luke 24:10, she was willing and eager to share the good news that Jesus had risen and was alive. Lastly, worship caused her to be baptized with the Spirit. She was more than likely among the unnamed women who were present in the upper room for the day of Pentecost in Acts 1:14. Paul declared in Romans 12:1 (ERV), "So I beg you, brothers and sisters, because of the great mercy God has shown us, offer your lives [a] as a living sacrifice to him—an offering that is only for God and pleasing to him." It's clear in my life that just like Mary of Magdala, I wanted to be where Jesus was and because I had chosen to follow Him, the course of my life was forever changed. The mercies of God delivered me from indwelling devils and my newfound love for God compelled me to give the best I had to offer: myself.

I began to faithfully attend a very good, Spirit filled, Bible teaching and preaching church that just so happened to be only minutes away from where I lived. The Holy Spirit would use my newfound church and pastor, my newly formed Christian relationships, and most importantly, what I did in my own home when no one was looking to teach me what it is to be a "true worshipper." This would become my lifestyle.

At church, the praise and worship were dynamic. Though the songs were all new to me, it didn't stop me from boldly singing along and, of course, weep anytime I felt the presence of God. I was a little awkward though, because I was surrounded by people, primarily women, where I sat and they all spoke in this strange language; they sang in it too. I wasn't afraid of it. Like I said, I wanted it all. I was intrigued.

For the first few weeks of regular attendance at church (Sunday mornings and evenings and Wednesday night Bible study), I pretty much absorbed the Word which was being preached. I observed everything happening around me during services, making mental notes. During praise and worship, people were free to walk up and down the aisles and in the pews with their hands raised upwards and I loved that. Some were even on their knees or were lying prostrate. I had never experienced this before; the thought of public worship was foreign to me and, quite frankly, a little intimidating.

My friend, Cyndi, introduced me to her friend, and she invited me to the church that I was now attending. She was a worshipper. When it came to really getting into the presence of God and losing herself in Him, she didn't care who was watching; she got her worship on. I wanted that. So, I began to fake it until I made it. Let me be clear, inwardly, I was sincere in my seeking God through worship; it was the outward actions that I'm referring to as "faking it." I hadn't quite learned that worship was indeed within me, so my focus was in expressing it from without.

During praise and worship services, I decided that I would keep my eyes on her and do everything she did. If she raised her hands, I raised my hands. If she walked the aisles, I did the same. If she dropped to her knees, I would fall to my knees. To this day, I don't know if she ever caught on to what I was doing. The thought of me mimicking my friend is a little funny, but hey, it worked. I will never forget the day when, after having a mighty anointed time during praise and worship, I got up off of my knees, wiped my eyes and nose, sat in my pew, and suddenly realized that I had done it on my own. An authentic worship had flowed out of me. I had not once looked at my friend for ideas to get into the presence of God. But ever since the music started, I had entered into a place in God from within myself and there I stayed lost in Him until the music stopped. The thought still moves me to this day. I had faked it, but now, I had made it and it was marvelous in my eyes.

I brought this style of worship home with me. Our choir had recorded a CD, so I bought one. For a while, this was the only gospel music I had. It didn't matter though. At five, and sometimes, four in the morning, it was "on and poppin" with praise and worship, me, my one CD, and the Lord. Every morning, my eyes would pop open at pretty much the same time and I would jump out of my bed eager to meet Jesus in my prayers and worship.

David said in Psalm 63:1 when he was in the desert, "O God, thou art my God; early will I seek thee: my soul thirsteth for thee, my flesh longeth for thee in a dry and thirsty land, where no water is." I had begun to develop the life habit of devoting the first few hours of my day to God. I realized I needed that fresh infilling from the well of living water that only the Holy Spirit could give me. I was getting something that no one or thing could give me, and it had nothing to do with a selfish prayer request to God. I just wanted to be in His presence, because therein was my joy. I was beginning to see the world around me as a dry land, so I turned my thirst for it towards Jesus. Morning by morning, as I honored His presence and acknowledged Him, my soul said, "Yes, Lord."

James 4:8 says to draw nigh to God and He will draw nigh to you. God was certainly keeping His promise. Those were some of the best days I had experienced in a while. In these times, I heard God call me by name for the first time and speak to me as if I was His daughter. While I would be lost in my thoughts of Him, He would show me the path of my life. Through visions and hearing His sweet voice, He would reveal His plans and purposes for my life. He would bring me back to my childhood memories, which were painful, and heal me of the hurt. He would also remind me of the times in my life where I triumphed and saw success, thus, healing me of the mindset of low self-esteem, unworthiness, and self-rejection. During these times, I began to get visions of myself behind a podium speaking or talking to a group of women about Christ. Besides acting, I was also a flower designer at the time and had my own business. God would give me witty ideas for new designs and show me better ways to handle business.

James 4:8 goes on to say, "Cleanse your hands, ye sinners; and purify your hearts, ye double- minded." The Lord would lovingly and gently show me things in my life that were not pleasing to Him. For example, I had fallen into my old habit of smoking again, after having been supernaturally delivered from that habit a few years earlier. Even though I wanted to stop, God began to show me that it was sin because I was leaning on cigarettes during stressful times in my life, instead of leaning on Him, and that's idolatry. In those moments of truth, all I could say was, "Yes, Lord. Please help me to make the necessary changes."

In the quiet moments of my devotion to God, He would reveal the filth in my heart, my thought life, and negative thinking. He was breaking up the fallow ground of my heart and getting it ready for planting His Word and will into it. On some mornings, all I could do was to put on a song and just sit at His feet, weeping and telling Him how much I loved and appreciated Him. It was especially in those moments that I felt like the poor sinner woman with her alabaster box of ointment; she loved on Jesus. Her sins were many, but she was forgiven of much and because she was forgiven of much, she loved much. She found Jesus in a house and began to weep at His feet. She used her tears and her hair to clean His feet and she anointed them with that beautiful fragranced oil (see Luke 36- 50). My worship was the sweet smelling fragrance that filled my home. I had been forgiven of all the sins and wrongdoings in my past and Jesus's sweet love towards me during those times of worship proved to me that I had been forgiven.

Eventually, my gospel music collection grew to three compact discs. A friend who found out that I had rededicated my life to Christ wanted to bless me, so he gave me a few of Hillsongs compact discs. By this time, I had turned the television off at my house and it stayed off for the next three years, unless I was watching the TBN Christian Network channel. I turned the radio off in my car as well. I would only listen to my pastor's sermons or one of my three compact discs from my music collection while driving. I was hungry and passionate for the things of God.

In a matter of just a few weeks, my lifestyle had dramatically changed. My private worship had spilled into my public life and the people close to me were beginning to see changes in me. I had made room for God in my everyday life and the payoff was wonderful. I attended church on a regular basis, participated in praise and worship at church and at home, had a growing prayer life and I read my Bible regularly. This was my worship to God. I was engaging in something that was paving the way for what would happen next.

Chapter Four

<u>Count the Cost: Commitment</u>

"And there went great multitudes with him: and he turned, and said unto them, 'If any man come to me, and hate not his father, and mother, and wife, and children, and brethren, and sisters, yea, and his own life also, he cannot be my disciple. And whosoever doth not bear his cross, and come after me, cannot be my disciple. For which of you, intending to build a tower, sitteth not down first, and counteth the cost, whether he have sufficient to finish it? Lest haply, after he hath laid the foundation, and is not able to finish it, all that behold it begin to mock him, Saying, This man began to build, and was not able to finish.'"
Luke 14:25-30

Within a month or two of my deliverance, I was in full revival. The fullness of the Godhead had come back to the center of my life, just where He belonged! I was on my way to forming the habit of faithfulness. I had been attending my new church on a regular basis. The Word of God was so rich that I had to keep coming back for more. Besides attending Sunday morning services (sometimes even the second service), I attended Wednesday night Bible study. I had even found an adult Sunday school class to attend on Sunday evenings, just before evening services. One might say that this was all a little radical, and I'm compelled to agree. I was radically thirsty and hungry for more of God. The more I received of Him only made me want more of Him. Call me greedy. I loved being in the atmosphere of worship, both at home and in church. Even though that fountain of living water within me was always overflowing, I still needed to drink more of the Spirit.

Nothing had changed circumstantially in my life at that point except my perspective, outlook of my life and the awareness that I now had of God. I continued going out on acting auditions on a regular basis, working as a flower designer and working my own flower business on the side. The nasty habit of smoking cigarettes had not changed either. I couldn't shake it. As much as I would pray and try to exercise self-control, nothing would give. I had been supernaturally delivered from a one pack a day cigarette habit a few years prior during a church service shortly after I was born again. It was Easter Sunday during resurrection service when I clearly remembered that while I was listening to the sermon, God's sweet calm voice came from within me, calling those things that be not as if they were, and said, "You stopped smoking." He spoke it to me as if I had already stopped. I responded positively and continued listening to the moving message of the cross. On that day, I had indeed stopped smoking. I lost my craving for cigarettes. I would be a non-smoker for more than two years.

One might ask how, after kicking a habit like that, would I choose to go back to it? Back then, I had not made an informed decision to follow Christ. My decision was based on the joy I felt upon my conversion experience. So even though I loved Him and I appreciated that I was sweetly saved, I didn't know enough about Him to be kept by Him. When the cares and storms of my life overwhelmed me, I didn't run to Jesus as I should have; I ran to cigarettes and other worldly comforts. Even though I made a decision to follow Him, I had little in me to cause me to remain faithful to the faith during times of trouble.

In Mark 4:14-20, Jesus teaches a parable describing four different conditions of the heart. These conditions prevent the Word of God from becoming rooted in us. He tells His disciples that man's heart is where the Word of God is planted; this helps believers to grow in faith, knowledge and understanding; this helps them to understand the ways of God. He describes a wayside condition where one hears the Word, and immediately, Satan comes and snatches it out of that person's heart. The second is a rocky soil where the believer hears the Word and immediately receives it with joy, but because he is not rooted in the Word when trouble or persecution comes, he doesn't last long. The third condition He describes is the thorny ground. In this, a man hears the Word, but it is quickly crowded out by the worries of life, the pursuit of wealth and the desire for the things of this world. Finally, there is good ground, where a man hears God's Word and accepts it. He then begins to produce multiplied fruit from the seed that was sown.

At the time of my conversion, the second and third conditions best describe the condition of my heart. Subsequently, I had only made a superficial commitment to becoming a Christian. I hadn't become someone who would follow Christ through thick or thin, rain or shine or sleet or snow yet. Frankly, I had heard the word "discipleship" in the new members' classes I'd taken a few years prior, but I didn't understand that I was to become one. Additionally, I didn't know that disciples needed to be disciplined. In true discipleship, God uses the troubles and cares of life to cause us to become rooted and grounded in the faith. Because I was still shallow in my faith, the cares and worries of this world distracted me from being able to grow in the faith.

Two years later, I found myself with a stronger addiction than before; the consequences of deciding to live life on my terms. I can confirm Jesus's teaching in Luke 11:24-26. He shared that when the wicked spirit is cast out, he comes back and finds the house is available for occupancy, but this time, he brings seven wicked spirits more evil than himself. This causes the last state of a man to be worse than the first. This described my present state. Since the time I picked up that first cigarette, lit it, inhaled and exhaled, I was pretty much in a full blown addiction again. It was as if I had picked up where I left off two years prior. Even after having been so dramatically delivered from the demons of shame, unworthiness and rejection about a month earlier, I was still dealing with the demons of addiction.

I was aggressive in trying to get free from this addiction before my re-dedication to the Lord. Even more so after my re-dedication since God began to deal with me about it in my prayer and worship time. Daily, I petitioned Him concerning this habit. I knew it wasn't pleasing to Him. I wanted out. I would stand before Him daily, dramatically admitting that I had willingly chosen to go back to this habit, but I could not willingly get myself out of it. I needed His help. I tried to control my urges to smoke, but to no avail. If I happened to be out of cigarettes and out running errands, I would not buy any on purpose, vowing that I would not smoke anymore after that day. Of course, that didn't work. At the first hint of a craving, I would stop what I was doing and head to the corner store for a pack of cigarettes. I was even willing to pay a much higher price at the corner store just to appease my addiction. After that pack was gone, I found myself making another commitment to stop smoking. When I was halfway through that pack of cigarettes, I would make another commitment to myself and God to quit. In addition to throwing away the remaining cigarettes of my current pack, I would twist them up before throwing them in the trash. As soon as my cravings were ignited again, I would find myself digging through the trash looking for pieces of twisted cigarettes to put back together. Once again, I would give in to my cravings and purchase another pack. This cycle repeated itself. I didn't stop at twisting the current cigarette pack before throwing it away, but I started to run water on them before throwing them in the trash. Who was I kidding? I found myself yet again not being able to keep the commitment to stop.

It was torture. I found no will-power within me to stop, even when every inhalation caused my throat to feel like it was on fire. I had to literally follow each exhalation with a sip of orange juice to sooth my throat. By this time, I had found the famous Bible teacher, Joyce Meyer, on TBN and I heard her testimony of quitting. I began to call those things that were not as though they were. When I found myself giving in to the craving, I began to repeatedly confess that I was a non-smoker in between puffs, just as she testified that she had done. I even fasted to try to break the addiction. It seemed nothing would work. I continued to do what I knew to do and that was to draw near to God and humble myself in His sight because, as the Bible says, He gives more grace to the humble (see James 4:6). I understood that I needed His grace. I would cry out to the Lord day and night, submitting myself to Him. I was determined and I was convinced that I would be free indeed.

Meanwhile, I had been on a steady pace of church attendance. This time around, something was different. I wasn't just attending church because it was the Christian thing to do. I was drawn now by the Word of God that I was hearing there and the lively worship of the praise team. Also, it was the love of God and the authentic intimate relationship with Him that I was growing in because of the worship, prayer, and study habits I had been forming at home. God was preparing me to be able to make the commitment to become a true disciple. Was I ready for the challenge?

At my church, I had begun to make some friends, especially with the women in the area I tended to sit. During one particular Sunday morning service, when the pastor had given an altar call, he also opened the doors of the church for anyone who wanted to become a member and make a deeper commitment to follow Jesus. A dear lady who often sat next to me nudged me, looked me right in my eyes and said, "You have been here for a while now. Don't you think it's about time you joined? You can't just continue to be a visitor." Joining the church was the last thing on my mind. Up until that point, it hadn't occurred to me that I should become a committed member. So, I just kindly smiled, nodded, looked away, and hoped that this moment would pass quickly.

I was the runaway bride. I loved being in a loving relationship both with God and with my new church family, but when it came to commitment, I didn't trust myself in that area. The answer for me was that I wasn't ready to make a commitment; the altar was not the place for me just yet. I didn't budge from that seat. In parting, my friend's words to me were, "Pray about it."

This was the same lady who had been instrumental in my getting filled with the Holy Spirit with the evidence of tongues just a few weeks earlier. One Sunday morning service during praise and worship, I had a perplexed look on my face because all the people were speaking and singing in their heavenly language. So, she walked up to me and said, "What these people are doing, I know this might look strange to you, but if you want this, He will give it to you. Just ask for it." Well, I did want it, so in that next moment, I simply said a prayer in my heart asking God to fill me. I don't know when it happened, but shortly thereafter, I began to speak in tongues, and from that time on, it became a regular part of my worship.

Because of this, I thought that I should give her suggestion to pray about joining the church some thought. Later that evening, I found myself contemplating my friend's suggestion to join the church. I began to have a conversation about it with the Lord. It went something like this. "Now Lord, we both know I don't do well with commitment. I've joined churches before and didn't stay and there have been many other situations to prove that I don't do well with commitment. My smoking habit is a good example. I think it's better to keep things the way they are. That way, there's no confusion; besides, I'm doing quite fine the way things are. Nevertheless, if You are asking me to join this church, then I will. Just order my steps, Lord." I can't say that I immediately got a response from the Lord. I just went on about my business and another week passed. At the end of the following Sunday service, when the pastor opened the doors of the church, with my friend cheering me on, I found myself rising out of my seat and walking down to the altar to accept the invitation. The Lord had given me an answer and was now ordering my steps.

I didn't know it at the time, but the Lord had a surprise blessing waiting for me on this very day. At the altar, the head altar worker instructed all those who had made a decision to join the church to follow her to a small room.

49

There, she gave us a nice welcome speech and handed out forms for us to fill out. She also gave instruction on what to do next in order to become an official member as well as information on the next new members' class. In closing, she asked if anyone had any prayer request. Immediately, the thought came to ask for prayer to stop smoking. However, my second thought was how embarrassed I'd be to admit to my habit. Out of about thirty or so of us in that room, no one said a word. Then I heard that little voice say to me, "You're going to miss out on your blessing." Immediately, I raised my hand. When called upon, I simply said that I wanted to stop smoking. In return, she said, "Oh, you just need to be delivered," implying that this was a small thing with God. Hands started going up after this, and after taking all the prayer requests, she made a simple prayer to God on behalf of all the new candidates for membership.

After the morning service, I went about my day and then returned for the evening service. During evening service, we had a guest speaker. I recognized him from seeing him on the Christian TV channel I had recently found. I have to admit that it was pretty exciting to see this televangelist at our church. From the very start of his message, he had my attention. He was preaching about Jesus being the great deliverer and how He wanted us free from the bondage of sin; his message was about getting free from addictions.

I was stirred and encouraged in my spirit because I was becoming convinced that God would do it for me. During his altar call, he began to call people to the altar if they wanted to be free. I believed that the altar call was for me. The evangelist started naming different addictions such as pornography, sexual addiction, cocaine and other drugs. When I heard this, my next thought was that I didn't want people to think I was addicted to that hard stuff... as if I never was. That was pride! Again, I heard that little voice say to me as He did on that morning, "You're going to miss out on your blessing." I jumped up immediately and ran down to the altar. There were hundreds of people at the altar. After the evangelist said a mighty prayer for all those wanting to be delivered of their addictions, he began to move throughout the crowd with much power. As a point of contact of faith, I was blessed that the man of God laid his hands on me. That sealed the deal for me as far as I was concerned.

That night, I slept peacefully. I didn't notice this at first, but I didn't need a cigarette before falling asleep. Now, this was a big deal because it was my custom to have a cigarette every night before falling asleep and the very first thing upon waking up in the morning. When I woke up the next morning, my first thought was that I needed a cigarette. The very next sound I heard was that little voice telling me, "No, you don't. You don't have any more desire for them; you are delivered." From that moment on, I haven't had another cigarette. I was free again. The day that I decided to make a deeper commitment to God, He decided that my trial of affliction was over. Again, because of my willingness and humility towards God, I had been freed from the tormenting spirit of addiction.

I've learned that God can do a lot with our willingness. Because I was willing, I went through with my commitment to become a full-fledged member of the church. This time, I completed the course because God's grace was on me, doing for me what I couldn't do for myself. For six straight weeks, I showed up for class with my homework completed. I can say that taking the class was beneficial to me; it was another step towards becoming rooted and grounded in God. God was now building me up on a strong foundation. I came to understand what was expected of me as a member, what the mission statement was, how important it was for me to understand the vision God had given our pastor for the ministry and what our particular church's purpose was in the community. Just as important, I came to understand that upon my decision to become a member, I was actually making a decision to become a disciple: a follower of Christ.

I was challenged to count the cost of discipleship. I needed to understand what I was making a commitment to. Jesus taught in Luke 9:23 that if anyone wanted to follow Him, they had to first deny themselves, that person had to take up his cross daily and follow Him. I was getting the picture. In counting the cost, I needed to forsake all my worldly goods and all of my earthly connections. It's not that I had to give up these things, but I had to let go of my emotional attachments so that these things had no power to hold me. Jesus said, "For where your treasure is, there will your heart be also" (Matthew 6:21).

I needed to know that God was expecting me to accept responsibility for where I was in life and to accept the trials and afflictions in my life as a cross I had to bear, instead of running away from them whenever I felt like giving up or when the going got too tough. If I could make a commitment to these things, I would be able to follow Jesus as a true disciple. Before the end of that class, I made a commitment to give my whole heart to God and the things of the kingdom. It wasn't a superficial commitment based on what Jesus could give me or do for me, but because of who He was. After all, He had the words of life. Where else could I go, or who else could I follow?

From the new members' class, God led me to take the altar workers' class so that I could begin to serve in my church. In a matter of just a few months, I had gone from being delivered from evil spirits and cigarettes to being filled with the Holy Spirit. Now, I was about to embark on yet another leg of my journey in Christ. This leg would prove to be vital to my functioning gifts, calling and purpose.

Chapter Five

<u>Grace: Growth: Power for Living</u>

"But grow in grace, and in the knowledge of our Lord and Savior Jesus Christ. To him be glory both now and forever. Amen."
2 Peter 3:18

Ephesians 2:8-9 says, "For by grace are ye saved through faith; and that not of yourselves: it is the gift of God: Not of works, lest any man should boast." In its simplest biblical definition, grace is unearned and undeserved favor from God to man for justification, sanctification, and salvation. God's divine favor and grace are exactly what was working in my life. God told Moses that He is gracious to whomever He chooses and will show mercy to whomever He chooses (see Exodus 33:19, Romans 9:15). My heart was full of gratitude that God saw it fit to show me His grace and mercy. I understood how much I was forgiven. Not by becoming consciously aware of every offense, sin or misdeed I had done in my life, but from the enormous amount of peace I had in my heart. The weight of sin, guilt, shame, and unworthiness had been removed. I was certainly appreciative of this unearned favor.

As a disciple of Christ, I was on my way to knowing this grace as more than the free gift unto salvation, but as the desire and the strength for living a life pleasing and dedicated unto God. The Greek word used for "grace" in Ephesians is "charis." The Blue Letter Bible website gives several definitions, one of which is "good will, loving-kindness and favor." Another definition is "of the merciful kindness by which God, exerting his holy influence upon souls, turns them to Christ, keeps, strengthens, increases them in Christian faith, knowledge, affection, and kindles them to the exercise of the Christian virtues." My favorite is, "the divine influence upon the heart, and its reflection in the life."

These definitions point to the function of the Holy Spirit in our lives. In Luke 9:23, Christ gave an instruction to His disciples by saying, "If any man will come after me, let him deny himself, and take up his cross daily, and follow me." If I was going to have any success in keeping Christ's instruction, I needed this grace working in my life. It would take the Holy Spirit Himself to exert the power and holy influence upon my heart in order to please God. I had tried to live life on my terms a few times; it didn't go so well. Fortunately for me, when I needed it most, I had this grace working in my life in a strong way and I'm convinced that it's what saved my life. Unfortunately, I didn't understand that it was God's grace, so eventually, I began to stray away from it, rather than to grow in it.

It was a few years earlier, almost immediately following that powerful time at the altar that I had gotten saved after my friend brought me to church with her. Afterwards, I went right back to the same lifestyle of smoking, drinking and drugging as if nothing had happened at the altar. Looking back, I can definitely testify that it was at that time that I began to lose the desire for those things. My lifestyle had not changed. I would still go to bars for drinks, drive drunk and go on wild searches for drugs in the middle of the night. Most nights, anyone could find me at some club in the bathroom stall snorting cocaine, and then drinking until I was in a blackout. This continued to some degree, even after I got saved and had given my life to Christ.

While nothing appeared to be different outwardly, something was certainly happening to me on the inside. I was actually losing the desire to do these things. At the time, the loss of desire made me miserable. I didn't understand it was the "divine influence" of God working on my heart because I had given Him permission to do so.

Night after night, I sat in the clubs drinking drinks that no longer did for me what they used to do; they didn't make me feel happy anymore. I would be out with the people I frequently partied with, but it was beginning to feel like they were strangers to me. I began to question why I was there because I really couldn't put my finger on the reason, but I no longer wanted to be there. I didn't know any other way at the time, so I just kept doing what I no longer wanted to do. I kept hanging out with the same crowd, going to the same clubs, drinking the same drinks and using the same drug, but none of it could do for me what it used to do.

God was changing my heart, but I kept pushing against the pricks. One night, after being out to score cocaine, I found myself at home alone drinking vodka directly from the bottle. I had used the cocaine I scored earlier, but it didn't get me high and I was miserably low. I felt so low that I wanted to end it all. I was just sick and tired of being sick and tired. What's even worse is that the Devil began to put thoughts in my head, saying things like, "You might as well end it all; you've made a mess of your life. There is no hope for you; there is no way to make anything out of your life at this point. End this life and you might have a chance to come back as a queen or something and have a better life."

The Devil was bluffing and I was buying into the lie yet again. In fact, since I came out of my mother's womb, the Devil had been trying to sabotage my life. Now, he was trying to end it. I had a brand new bottle of extra strength pain pills and there were over 200 pills in the bottle. I broke the seal, opened the lid, poured about 80 tablets into my hand and took them. I don't remember what I used to wash them down with; maybe it was the bottle of vodka if it hadn't been emptied by then. I remember smiling afterwards; I don't know why. Maybe, it was because I expected the pain to go away. I don't know how much time passed, but it seemed like hours later when I woke up out of sheer darkness to my own blood-curdling scream. The scream was so loud that my neighbor knew something was wrong and came right over. Thankfully, she had a key to my front door. The pain was horrible and my neighbor didn't try talking to me; she just called 911.

At the hospital, I was given intravenous treatment since the pills had already dissolved in my system; they knew this by the level of pain that I was in. God showed His favor and mercy to me that night. How else can one explain why my liver did not fail or I didn't die from poison? By His great mercy, He saw it fit to intervene and without my expectation, He was getting ready to destroy the enemy of addiction.

I found myself admitting my intentions to harm myself to the hospital personnel. That admission coupled with the fact that there was cocaine found in my blood stream, guaranteed me a bed at the psych ward. I didn't know this at the time, but the doctor in charge of the psych ward would not be releasing me until I was able to face the fact and admit that I was an addict. It took a full seven days of half-hour meetings for me to understand that my life was miserable and out of control because I used drugs and alcohol, and not the other way around.

From the time I was admitted, I would be summoned to the psychiatrist's office each morning. There, he would sit behind his desk, and in a calm voice, he would ask me the same simple question: "Why are you here?" On the first visit, I remember thinking to myself before answering, "Oh, this will be easy." After that, I proceeded to explain to him that it was because my mother had a nervous breakdown when I was young, which I never quite recovered from and she had been diagnosed with manic depression and schizophrenia.

Plus, my father had been a heroine addict who had been in and out of prison most of my life. After a few minutes of talking, he would promptly excuse me until the following day. On the next morning, after having been asked the same question in the same manner as the previous morning, I gave yet another answer which I believed to be the reason. I explained that when I was young, I was sexually molested and raped. On the third day, the question was the same, and I probably responded by saying something about when I was in college, I had an abortion and since then, I'd had several more. His response was always the same until the last visit. I believe that what made the difference in this last visit was what happened the night before.

It was during recreation time when all the patients were in the common area. Suddenly, some "volunteers" arrived and were going around the room making small talk with the patients. I was sitting alone and an enormous amount of paranoia and fear suddenly came upon me. I had experienced paranoia before, but only while I was using. However, I had never experienced it at the level I was experiencing it at, and at that point, I hadn't used drugs in at least six days. I remember feeling like I didn't want to make eye contact with anyone. I thought that everyone in that room would try to harm me in some way, whether it was a "volunteer," a patient or hospital personnel. It definitely was not a pleasant experience.

Finally, one of the "volunteers" made her way to where I was sitting. She was pleasant in her manner when she explained to me that there would be a "meeting" taking place in a few minutes to which I was invited if I felt up to it. Of course I did. I would have done anything to get out of that atmosphere of fear. As it turned out, the "volunteers" were a group of people with at least one thing in common: drugs! They were all recovering addicts. The one peculiar thing that stood out to me was that before each began to share their story of recovery, they would say their first name only and then speak the tag line, "I'm an addict." I hadn't heard of Narcotics Anonymous (NA) up until that point in my life, however, over the course of the meeting, as the "volunteers" shared their experiences of drug usage, I remember connecting to what most of them were sharing. This particular meeting focused on the first three steps of the twelve steps to recovery, which both the AA (Alcoholics Anonymous) and NA programs are founded upon. This meant that while I was hearing and connecting to their stories, I was also hearing the solution to my addiction. If I wanted recovery, all I would need to do is to take the first three simple steps to recovery as they did.

First, I would need to admit that I was powerless over cocaine and that my life had become unmanageable. Secondly, I had to believe that there was a power greater than myself who could restore me to sanity, and finally, I would need to make a decision to turn my will and my life over to the care of God. At the end of that meeting, the leader invited anyone else to share. I really didn't know what to share, but I found that when I opened my mouth what came out was, "I'm an addict." In that moment, I realized how much shame I had been carrying and how much of a burden it had been to keep the secret of my drug use; a secret that really wasn't a secret at all. Almost everyone who knew me, knew that I was using.

Additionally, I came to realize that my life was out of control and miserable, but not because of where I had come from in life or what injustices I endured, but because of the choices I made in my life. One of those choices was to use drugs. Cocaine had the upper hand in my life; I was enslaved to it. I tried to stop using numerous times, but I'd failed miserably. Now, my trust was in God as I made the decision to give my will and life over to Him.

I was thankful for His grace. What the enemy tried to use to destroy me, God used for my good. Just days earlier, I had been so sick of living that I wanted to die and I nearly did. Now, in a psychiatric hospital, I saw hope in living for the very first time in a long time. I saw what I was clearly, and more importantly, I was finally willing to admit it, making no excuses. If I had known to sing, I would have sung "Amazing grace! How sweet the sound that saved a wretch like me! I once was lost, but now am found; was blind, but now I see. 'Twas grace that taught my heart to fear, and grace my fears relieved; how precious did that grace appear the hour I first believed. Through many dangers, toils and snares, I have already come; 'Tis grace hath brought me safe thus far, and grace will lead me home."

When I went out into the common area after the meeting, I remember first that the paranoia was gone and then, the sense of relief I felt. I could make eye contact with people again. The paranoia was gone because shame had been removed, and shame had been removed because I had faced the truth. Grace opened my eyes to the truth. God simply used the NA meeting and the people in attendance to help me to see the truth and the truth made me free. The next morning, after the doctor asked me the same question, "Why are you here?" my immediate response was to look him in his eyes and without hesitation, say to him just four little words: "Because I'm an addict." He put his pen down, sat back in his chair and began to discuss my case of addiction with me.

From my release date until this very day, I have not had one struggle with cocaine ever again. No craving, no desire. I stood strong even when a friend who I had naively told that I kicked the habit tried to tempt me into using with him. On the pretense of celebrating with me, he styled my hair free of charge. I noticed that when I arrived at his salon, there were no other clients there. I was his last customer of the day. When he finished my hair, he announced that he had a surprise for me. He momentarily stepped into a back room and reappeared with a huge mirror with lots of cocaine poured on top of it. I guess God had to show me that truly His "divine influence" working upon my heart had set me free and that I was no longer under the oppression of the enemy. I said to him, "No, I don't want that." And the Holy Spirit was present in me affirming that I meant it. My friend and the Devil would learn on that night that I was free; I learned this lesson too. The Holy Spirit gave me grace enough to stand up and walk out without looking back!

Life was different without the bondage of cocaine to struggle with, but it wasn't enough with God; He wanted it all. I still had an addiction to alcohol that He would open my eyes to. Unbelievably, I didn't think I had a problem with alcohol, so after getting released from the hospital, I continued to frequent bars for drinks. The only difference was that I was no longer in the bathroom stalls snorting cocaine.

I still did not find any pleasure in being in the bars; I just didn't know what else to do. I was lonely and without true direction and purpose. I was chasing my dreams my way on my terms because I had no sense of purpose. What I know now is that I never had to chase the dream. When I began to chase God, purpose came to me, but it would be yet a few more seasons in my life before I would come to understand this.

Nevertheless, the grace of God continued to order my steps, and this time, it was in the form of a driving under the influence (DUI) charge. I thought it was just my dumb luck that I was in another dilemma. I was now facing jail time because I got caught driving drunk not long after I had been released from the hospital. The blessing for me was that because His grace was at work, there were just some things that I could no longer get away with... one of those things being driving drunk. After a night in jail, and then, facing the judge, I was pretty much scared straight. In court, the judge had mercy on me. This was my second DUI, and instead of receiving a sentence of jail time, the judge spoke to me from his bench. He said in a stern voice as if I were his daughter or loved one, "Young lady, I don't want to see you dead in a ditch somewhere. I'm giving you a fine of one thousand dollars, I'm putting you on probation for a period of one full year, and I'm going to make it mandatory that you do '90 AA meetings in 90 days'. If you do not complete the '90 in 90,' you will spend the remainder of your probation time behind bars. Your probation officer who will be assigned to you before leaving this courthouse today, will explain the details."

I didn't know what "90 in 90" was, but I was willing to do whatever it took to stay out of jail. My probation officer explained that "90 in 90" referred to attending Alcoholics Anonymous (AA) meetings every day for a period of 90 days. I objected with a strong outburst, "What! I'm an actress! What if I get a job out of town? I wouldn't have to attend on those days that I was working, right?" I was looking for her agreement. I didn't get a response, so I concluded by telling her that the court ordered arrangement would not work for me and to just let me pay the fine of one thousand dollars then I could be on my way. She replied just as firmly, but with a lot more control, since the judge and God were on her side. She said something like, "Young lady, AA is nationwide, and I suggest you keep this list of meetings held in every state handy, because the other option for you is jail time." She continued to "lay down the law" by informing me of how I would further be inconvenienced. I would have to come to her office on a weekly basis with proof of my attendance and if I let the sun go down on one day without having attended a meeting, I would be put in jail. I had exactly thirty days to begin my meetings. Of course, within that thirty days, I drank. I had every intention of going to those meetings because jail was not an option for me. I was very afraid of going to jail and God knew it. But I was going to stretch my luck. I decided that I would begin the meetings exactly on the thirtieth day.

But God! He had a plan all along. It was within those thirty days that I got delivered from alcohol in much of the same way as I did cocaine. God brought me to the truth about myself; I was an alcoholic. My deliverance came because I became willing to admit it out loud to someone other than myself. I can't say that it was because I just got tired of the guilt and treacherous hangovers I had to live with after each night of binge drinking until I passed out. Those things helped, but if that were the case entirely, I would have been free long before those DUI charges. Since I couldn't drive drunk anymore, I was drinking at home alone, and God was tugging on my heart with every beer can I emptied and threw out. Alone, I was forced to look at my life and myself and admit that I didn't like what I saw. I had recently broken a promise to my nephew who I cared deeply for. After a night of drinking alone, I passed out and slept until the middle of the next day, missing our date at the puppet show that I promised to take him to. Additionally, I had recently worked on a print ad which I was almost fired from because I arrived on the set still drunk from the night before. I began to see that God was not pleased with my life and neither was I. Finally, I had just been cast to work on a short film that my acting coach had suggested me for. I was given the opportunity to do what I loved to do and I knew nothing good could come from drunkenness. I had come to the conclusion that I would have to give up alcohol for life and I realized I couldn't do it on my own, after all, I had tried and failed miserably. I would need help. With tears streaming down my face, I looked up toward heaven and sincerely said a simple prayer, "God, I need your help." The last day that I woke up from a blackout with a hangover was the day God impressed upon my heart to go to the house of a person whose friendship and respect I valued. There I stood in the middle of his living room, announcing that I was an alcoholic and that though I couldn't imagine my life without it, I knew I needed to give it up. I told him that when I would start attending the AA meetings, I was going with the intention of getting free and that I would trust God to help me to do so.

That's all God needed: my willingness to stand up and to say it out loud! On the thirtieth day which was the day that I began the meetings, I was already about a week sober and never again did I have to struggle with the addiction of alcohol or cocaine. On my road to deliverance from substance abuse, grace was my faithful friend, "standby" and "strength." He was my "good will, loving-kindness and favor" in the clubs when I didn't want to be there, on that awful night that could have been fatal, in the psych ward and when I had to face the judge. He was that "divine influence upon the heart" convincing me to face the truth about myself and to choose life rather than death. Finally, it was by His wonderful message of grace on that resurrection Sunday morning that I received my supernatural deliverance from cigarettes.

I had grown up in the church, and several of my family members were praying people; some were even preachers. One of my fondest memories of having been in the church as a child was on Sunday mornings, hearing my granddaddy, Walter Love's passionate prayers. Up until this point, I had never seen a grown man weep. He served as a faithful deacon of the church and when called upon, he would slide off the front row pew where he sat, get down on one knee and would call to "the God in heaven; his merciful Father" on behalf of his pastor, church, and family. He would call the presence of God into the church as he asked God to take notice of his wife, sons, daughters-in-law, his nieces and nephews and grandchildren. As a woman of God today, I praise God for the faithfulness of my maternal grandmother, Almeda Bates (Nanny, as we called her), who raised my siblings and I. Surely, it was only by the grace of God that this elderly widow would get five children through school and into their adulthood. She would do so by trusting God. She was a woman of faith. She would make sure that every Sunday morning, we would have a few coins in our hands for the offering and whether she could make it to church or not, she would see to it that we were on that church van.

Back then, I had accepted Christ as my personal Savior mostly because of these godly examples and their faithfulness. Unfortunately, by the time I reached a certain age, I began to drift away from God. It was probably because I hadn't entered into a close personal relationship with Christ. When I began to make major mistakes in my life, I thought God was mad at me and that I had no right to run to Him. I found myself empty, alone, and addicted. I knew to call to God, after all, I was raised in the church, but what kept me from going to Him was the hopeless guilt I felt for leaving Him. All the while, His great love, mercy, and grace compelled Him to leave the other ninety-nine sheep to come and look for the one lost sheep: me (see Luke 15:4).

When I needed Him most and didn't know how to return to Him, He came and rescued me. It was His compassion flowing from my friend that compelled her to drive out of her way on that Sunday morning to bring me to church. She knew that I was hurting, and she understood that only God could fix me. It was His hand in her hand holding my hand as she walked with me down to that altar because I needed to say the sinner's prayer and give my life back to God.

It was from the prayers of the saints of old, including my granddaddy, Walter Love and my Nanny Bates who prayed in advance, asking God to remember their prayers and have mercy on me, their loved one even before I fell. It was simply by His grace that He chose to have mercy and show favor to me and that's what brought me back into fellowship with God. I was headed towards full restoration of mind, body, and soul. I was right where I needed to be, and I'm sure I pledged my unfailing love and my complete obedience to God for the rest of my life.

However, not soon after I began to recover in life, I began to backslide. Yep, I came crawling back to God in the middle of my misery, and then when things got better I forgot how much I needed Him and what He'd actually saved me from. I didn't know then that it was good for me to be back in the church because being back meant being back in the middle of God's will for my life. If I was back in His will, I was on the correct road to true purpose and destiny. If I was on that road, it could only mean that I was growing as a true disciple of Christ. If I was growing as a true disciple, that would mean that God, by His grace, would change my life, not just for a season, but for a lifetime. Unfortunately, I began to assume that I didn't need so much church or God, so eventually, I began to drift away from those opportunities. If I had known better, I would not have had to live under the bondage of addiction or bear the torturous yoke of the enemy for so long.

There I was again, having been delivered from demons, dedicated back to God and benefiting from His grace, only this time, I knew intuitively that I had been trying to work out my life in my own strength. I knew that I no longer had to do so. I had help in the form of divine grace! In Matthew 11:28-30, Jesus said "Come unto me, all ye that labour and are heavy laden, and I will give you rest. Take my yoke upon you, and learn of me; for I am meek and lowly in heart: and ye shall find rest unto your souls. For my yoke is easy, and my burden is light." Jesus gave a call to people who were trying to bear the burdens of this life in their own strength.

He instructed them to take His yoke, reassuring them that it would be easy and light. I had entered that rest Jesus spoke of and was now reacquainted with the yoke of the divine grace abiding in me.

I also knew intuitively that the key to continuing on this newfound road of peace was in growing in this grace, and in the knowledge of our Lord and Savior, Jesus Christ. This time, I had stuck around long enough to finish the new members' class, and now, this same "divine influence" would lead me to take the altar workers' class.

I really enjoyed this class, but it was intense. It required a lot of scripture memorization and study in the areas of salvation, God's love and being filled with the Holy Ghost. Within a few short weeks, we learned how to lead others to Christ through the sinners' prayer and to scripturally minister salvation and assurance of salvation. We were also trained to lead others to be filled with the Holy Spirit and to minister this through the scriptures.

I took this class seriously. I saw it as an honor to serve God in this way, however, I have to admit that I struggled with whether or not I would be able to serve others in such a way. I didn't believe I was qualified because of where I had come from in my life and the fact that I was a baby Christian myself. Throughout the class, the instructor continually reassured us that as long as we put in the work and were sincere in our commitment, that the Holy Spirit would not abandon us, but would be leading us as we served. The thought of going to the altar during altar call on the Sundays that I would serve was very intimidating, but there was no way around it. The conviction and desire in my heart to serve in this capacity would not keep me from it.

Graduation finally came and brought with it the time to officially serve as an altar worker in the mega church I was attending. There were over 8,000 members at that church and I felt like a baby eagle whose mother had just pushed it out of the nest. Nevertheless, I would soon see this energizing, miraculous power of grace at work through me in the sweetest way. At the appropriate time, I walked down to the altar and stood directly in back of a young lady who had tears streaming down her cheeks. I felt the leading of the Holy Spirit within me as I gently put my hand on her shoulders to let her know that she was not alone. I was settled; I knew that it was God's hand in my hand that was leading her to the area where she would be ministered to. As I opened my mouth to reassure her of this wonderful grace, it was God's voice in my voice comforting her. What better way to begin the journey of growing in this wonderful grace than by the very thing in which I had been called to: ministry!

Chapter Six

Parakletos: The Person of the Holy Spirit: With Me

"And I will pray the Father, and he shall give you another Comforter, that he may abide with you for ever; even the Spirit of truth; whom the world cannot receive, because it seeth him not, neither knoweth him: but ye know him; for he dwelleth with you, and shall be in you."
John 14:16

In Romans 5:5, Paul teaches us that God's love has been poured out in our hearts by the Holy Spirit, who has been given to us. I have grown to know the person of the Holy Spirit as such a gentle, peaceful being. In my quietest moments, it was as if I could actually feel and hear another heartbeat within myself. I really can't say that I had one of those "aha" moments to where I got a clear revelation of who the Holy Ghost is. For me, I gradually got to know and understand Him over a period of time. I did know this right away: I was not alone and that I was loved.

The love of God which was afforded to me was now more personal and intimate. Up until this point in my life, I had only a head knowledge of God's love for me. I knew that He loved me, but only saw it as a love coming from without. Something was different this time. Through the person of the Holy Spirit in me, it was tangible and I was beginning to understand that there is a love that comes from within and it made me want more. God will most certainly give us more of His Holy Spirit when we ask for Him to do so in prayer (see Luke 11:12-13).

One day, while in my personal prayer time, I asked God to let me experience His love. During that time of prayer, the Holy Spirit brought me to the apostle Paul's prayer in Ephesians 3:17-20. So I began to pray daily that I would come to understand how wide, how long, how high and how deep His love is, and I didn't stop there. I also began to ask to experience His love in every way that I could think of. I said to God, "Let me hear Your love, feel Your love, taste Your love, smell Your love and understand Your love. I would ask Him to give me a revelation of His love, let me see His love, let me walk in His love and let me breathe His love.

I believe that the manner of my prayer to God concerning His love was instrumental in some way to my coming to know who the Holy Spirit is. Soon after, I began to experience what I thought at the time was a phenomenon; the presence of the person of the Holy Spirit in a consistent manner in my everyday life. Since the Holy Spirit is God and God is love, it makes sense that I was suffocated in His love. His perfect love was casting out fear. I felt accepted, safe, and peaceful. Day after day, the Holy Spirit's comforting assurance was there encouraging me to grow deeper in this love that was so lavishly being bestowed upon me.

I know now that what I was experiencing was no phenomenon. The Holy Spirit's presence in my life is the very proof of my salvation. He is the "seal," the very proof that I am owned and protected by God. Ephesians 1:13 (AMP) reads, "In Him, you also, when you heard the word of truth, the good news of your salvation, and [as a result] believed in Him, were stamped with the seal of the promised Holy Spirit [the One promised by Christ] as owned *and* protected [by God]."

I had been baptized in this very Spirit as well! He was the "promise of the Father" whom Jesus spoke of in Luke 24:49 to be poured upon us for power, witnessing, and living for God. In fact, at the end of His earthly ministry, Christ began to talk about the Holy Spirit to His followers. He promised that the Holy Spirit would be sent in His place as another comforter, and that He, the Holy Spirit, would abide with us forever and would be in us (see John 14:16-17).

The Greek word that Jesus used for "comforter" is "parakletos." *Vine's Complete Expository Dictionary* provides the following explanation for the word. It means "called to one's side" or "called to one's aide." It was used in a court of justice to denote a legal assistant, counsel for the defense, an advocate; one who pleads another's cause before a judge. An intercessor or an advocate. I love the *Amplified Bible's* version because it brings the word "comforter" out in a very practical manner for all to understand. It reads as follows, John 14:16 (AMP), "And I will ask the Father, and He will give you another Comforter (Counselor, Helper, Intercessor, Advocate, Strengthener, and Standby), that He may remain with you forever."

Notice also that this passage of scripture records Jesus as saying that He would ask the Father to send "another" comforter. According to the *Vine's Complete Expository Dictionary*, the word "another" in the Greek, "allos," implies "another of the same sort" and not another as in different. In this sense, Christ served as the "Comforter" to all that followed Him in His day, especially the twelve apostles, whom He drew close to Him, teaching them about the kingdom of God and of their salvation which was to come. In their day, the apostles and those who followed Jesus faced persecution, humiliation, fearful circumstances, rejection and more, but He was there with them, consoling them. Jesus taught them about the kingdom of God. He performed miracles of healing and other great works, revealing the power of God. He told them about His Father in heaven, He gave them instruction on how they should live, and He was a part of their everyday lives. He was their peace, Emmanuel (God with them), and finally, in the finished work of the cross, He was their legal "assistance" to God's righteousness.

When He was ready to go to the cross, Jesus sensed the fear and sorrow that filled His disciples' hearts and began to comfort them by explaining that His Spirit would be sent to function just as He had in their lives. In essence, He was telling them that their lives would be even better because now, they would have Him, not just "with" them but "in" them (see John 16:7; 14:17). This promise is not just for the disciples and followers of Christ in that day, but for all who will put their faith and trust in Christ today. Acts 2:39 says it best, "For the promise is unto you, and to your children, and to all that are afar off, even as many as the Lord our God shall call."

I'm sure glad I answered the call; I'm only sorry that it took so long in my Christian life to understand this. Christ's Spirit, the Holy Spirit with me was sent from the Father because of the finished work of the cross.

He's here to walk alongside me and talk with me and to help me through the trials and tribulations of this life here on earth. No wonder Jesus said such things to His disciples as, "These things I have spoken unto you, that in me ye might have peace. In the world ye shall have tribulation: but be of good cheer; I have overcome the world" (John 16:33). "...Let not your heart be troubled, neither let it be afraid" (John 14:27), and "I will not leave you comfortless: I will come to you" (John 14:18). He went on to explain in John 14:19 that in that day of the finished work, "... ye shall know that I am in my Father, and ye in me, and I in you." In Christ, we have the fullness of God because we have the "promise of the Father" in us! This is why my new anthems in life had become, Galatians 2:20, "I am crucified with Christ: nevertheless I live; yet not I, but Christ liveth in me...," and I John 4:4, "...greater is he that is in you, than he that is in the world."

I took these promises personally; they became a part of my daily confessions. It was my way of reminding myself that I had the life of God in me through the abiding presence of the Holy Spirit. My old self was gone. I was a new creature in Christ and dedicated to God. Through the person of the Holy Spirit, I had the power and love of God in order to live for Christ! His Spirit had taken up residence in the core of my being and very much wanted to express Himself through me.

It was vitally important that I get to know this "Comforter" since He was now in charge of my life. I had committed to being a follower of Christ, but that didn't necessarily mean that I was a follower of Christ. It would take the discipleship of the Holy Spirit to teach me and to help me keep my commitment to becoming a true follower of Christ. In other words, if I lived in the Spirit, I had to learn to walk in the Spirit. John 2:6 states, "He that saith he abideth in him ought himself also so to walk, even as he walked." It was important that I get to know Him who would lead me for the rest of my life. The presence of the Holy Spirit in me was bearing witness that indeed I was a child of God, and the love was confirming acceptance rather than rejection. I John 4:13 reads, "Hereby know we that we dwell in him, and he in us, because he hath given us of his Spirit."

In chapters 14-16 of the book of John, Christ gives beautiful explanations of some of the attributes of the Holy Spirit. John 14:17 (AMP) records that the Holy Spirit is, "The Spirit of Truth, whom the world cannot receive (welcome, take to its heart), because it does not see Him or know and recognize

Him. But you know and recognize Him, for He lives with you [constantly] and will be in you." The Holy Spirit is "The Spirit of the Truth," since He is Christ's Spirit. Christ is the Word made flesh and the Word is God's truth. I couldn't be a disciple without God's Word; the Holy Spirit would reveal it to me. In verse 26 of the same chapter, Jesus declared that the Holy Spirit would teach the disciples all things and bring back to their remembrance the things that Jesus taught them. In John 16:13, Jesus tells us that the Holy Spirit is the one who "will guide you into all truth." The Holy Spirit would reveal God's Word to me, teach me it and remind me of it through my daily walk in life.

The abiding presence of the Holy Spirit also brought an abiding love for the Word of God. I couldn't get enough of it. It became a part of my life in a big way. I took my Bible with me into worship in the mornings, in my prayer closet; it went with me in my car, to work, to the set when I was working and, of course, to church. In a nutshell, everywhere I was, my Bible was. I opened it up and read it whenever I could. Daily, I couldn't wait to get home to get in the Word of God.

This was another aspect of God's love working in my life. He was giving me a hunger and love for His Word. I found that I could understand it too. I had recently been baptized in the Holy Spirit and had the evidence of speaking in tongues. I noticed that my basic Bible reading was different from this point. It was like putting on those special glasses to watch a

3D movie. Beforehand, I kind of struggled when reading; it felt like being in a 3D movie without the glasses. When viewing a 3D movie, you can still see the movie without the glasses, but with the glasses, the experience is so much more profound and exciting and you certainly don't miss any of the subtle nuances of the movie. The Holy Spirit brought the aspect of the "living Word" to me in this way. Rather than just reading the words, the Spirit was giving me revelation knowledge of what I was reading.

Additionally, after reading even for a short period of time, I literally felt fueled up. I felt like I wanted to do something like climb a mountain, run a mile or conquer the world. The Word gave me so much hope, inspiration, motivation and joy. I remember when I began to use cocaine, I would feel like that after taking a hit. Of course, at the end of my addiction, it wasn't like that. This only proved the fact that what is not good for you may appear to be good for a season, but when it's not of God, the end of that road is always destruction.

Regarding my addiction to cocaine and alcohol, I found that I had been self-medicating. The symptoms were depression, rejection and the like, and I had been taking Satan's counterfeit prescription for my ailments. I had also been taking huge doses of the world and all that was in it! The Bible teaches us that it is the Word of God which brings healing to our souls and so the Word of God had become my new prescription to a happy life. It brought joy, peace, health, and freedom. Psalm 107:20 says this about God, the Father: "He sent his word, and healed them, and delivered them from their destructions." Jesus is the Word that was sent and the Word was made flesh (see John 1:14). Jesus said, "… the words that I speak unto you, they are spirit, and they are life" (John 6:63). I added the living Word of God to my daily spiritual diet and because the Word is alive, it began to change my thinking, actions and the course of my life. Cocaine and alcohol brought chaos and death, but the Word of God was bringing life and that more abundantly. The Holy Spirit was right there every day to guide me to the truth in the written word, which was and is my daily dose of "spiritual bread." Jesus said that man should not live by natural bread only, but by every word that proceeds out of the mouth of God (see Matthew 4:4). He would lead me to the scriptures that were relevant to what I would face in my daily living and what He was doing in me to change and conform me to the image of Jesus.

Change of mind was coming too because of what I was doing with the Word. I wasn't just reading it, but I was also meditating on it and confessing it. Proverbs 4:20-22 reads, "My son, attend to my words; incline thine ear unto my sayings. Let them not depart from thine eyes; keep them in the midst of thine heart. For they are life unto those that find them, and health to all their flesh." When the second generation of the Israelites were getting ready to go into the promised land to dwell, God gave their new leader, Joshua, the following instructions: Joshua 1:8 reads, "This book of the law shall not depart out of thy mouth; but thou shalt meditate therein day and night, that thou mayest observe to do according to all that is written therein: for then thou shalt make thy way prosperous, and then thou shalt have good success." The Holy Spirit taught me how to meditate on the scriptures because He wanted to renew my thinking.

He would meet me in my prayer closet as I confessed the Word out loud over myself, after all, there is power and life in the spoken Word of God. I began to write the scriptures on post-it notes and would post them all over the walls of my house so that I could be reminded of what I was reading. I would write scriptures on index cards so that I was able to have quick access when I was at a red light while driving, and when I would take "prayer walks," so that I could confess the Word.

I will never forget the moment when I recognized the benefit of "hiding the word in my heart." I was praying to God about my finances in the middle of one of my prayer walks. I heard the voice of Satan. I know it was him because when he opens his mouth, he lies and what he said to me was a lie. Out of nowhere, I heard a voice say something to the effect of, "There is a lot of money in this world, but not enough, so therefore, you will never have enough." This was something I often heard Satan say to me since childhood. Sadly, I bought into the lie. However, this time, the next voice immediately following it was the voice of the Holy Spirit speaking through me! What came out of my mouth was, "My God shall supply all of my needs according to His riches and glory by Christ Jesus. He gives me power to gain wealth! He shall cause men to give into my bosom because I am an obedient giver and tither!" These were scriptures I had been meditating on. Like David, the Word was hid in my heart and when Satan came to tempt me into doubt and unbelief, the Holy Spirit brought to my remembrance in its proper context, what Christ said in His Word concerning me. His truth rose up to demolish the stronghold of lack and the mindset of poverty.

This manner of prayer and daily declarations would prove to be key in changing my thinking in many areas of my life. When I needed healing from a painful herniated disc in my neck and back, the Holy Spirit led me to write prayers filled with healing scriptures from the Word to declare over myself and to build my faith. I learned that the hearing of the Word builds faith! I began to preach to myself and to my body! When the surgeon told me that I needed to have surgery right away or else I would have permanent nerve damage, I believed the "report of the Lord" that I had been meditating on and chose not to have the surgery. To this date, I am free of the excruciating back pain that once made my life so miserable and I have the proper use of all of my limbs. I was overcoming by learning to have faith in the Word of God through the help of the Holy Spirit!

I was also learning to trust God and His careful watchfulness over me as I simply meditated on scriptures that the Holy Spirit would lead me to. I remember for weeks, I had been appropriating the blood of Jesus over myself through confessing scriptural prayers I had written. One day, I was driving around town running errands and was stopped at a traffic light when a strong presence of the Holy Spirit flooded my car, bringing me into a trance. My eyes fixed on all the people in the city streets scurrying about taking care of their business, and at that very moment, I could faintly sense a glass wall or covering around me. Not in a bad sense; however, I felt separated from them all. Some of the people had their own coverings, but I could only sense mine. I could hear the voice of the Spirit saying things like "The blood protects," "The blood sanctifies and separates you," "The blood keeps you safe" and "You are under my pavilion." It was a marvelous moment of literally feeling the reality of the covering of the blood. I felt so privileged that I was a child of God and loved. Romans 8:16 promises us that the Spirit bears witness with our spirit that we are children of God!

There were many times of correction as well. Hebrews 12:6 (NIV) says, "Because the Lord disciplines the one he loves, and he chastens everyone he accepts as his son." I was beginning to understand how the Holy Spirit wanted to lead me to situations where the outcome would be that I would see the condition of my heart and what God wanted to correct. For example, during this time in my life, I was getting a lot of traffic tickets and violations. Everything from speeding, making illegal turns and parking in no parking zones. My mindset at the time was: *A girl gotta do what a girl gotta do in order to make it to that audition on time.* I was spending hundreds of dollars on tickets, thinking this was just the cross I had to bear. I had just received yet another ticket, and this one came through the mail. This time, my reaction was grief to the point where I shed tears of anger and frustration. I guess I was upset because I didn't see this one coming. Unbeknownst to me, the city had recently installed a red light camera at an intersection that I frequently ran red lights at. The citation included a clear picture of me in my car leaned over my steering wheel looking like I was trying to make my car go faster in order to beat the red light. The only problem was the picture clearly showed that the light was already red when I chose to run it, and in the picture, my lips were perfectly formed so that you could interpret the cuss word about to come out. This proved that I was very much aware of what I was doing at the time! Yep, I was a Christian, filled with the Holy Ghost, tongue talking and Bible toting. What made matters worse was when a friend told me that all I had to do was go to court and contest the ticket with the complaint that the camera must have malfunctioned, but "conviction" wouldn't allow me to as much as I wanted to. All I had to do was demand that I have a right to face my accuser as he had recently done and won. I found that I couldn't bring myself to do it, even with the firsthand knowledge that the judge would have to throw it out of court on the basis that you couldn't get a camera to come to court to testify against you.

I actually considered going to court with this argument for a moment, even though I knew this meant that I would have to say I didn't run a red light. I couldn't do that for two reasons. First, the strong conviction that was in my heart because I knew that I had run the red light. The picture was clear; it was me and the light was red. Secondly, the strong conviction that was on me because God knew it wasn't true. The Holy Spirit used the occasion to remind me of the very moment that picture was taken. He reminded me of what I was thinking and how the word that came out of my mouth in that moment sounded.

The Holy Spirit does have a way of showing us the truth about ourselves. So honestly, I was afraid to face the judge because I had a fear of God. Instead, the Holy Spirit prompted me to go and ask one of my Christian friends (who was actually my mentor) to pray for me. After I told her what had happened and that I felt led to have her pray for me, I then proceeded to ask her to pretty much pray away the consequences, and that's when things got pretty sticky. She agreed to pray for me, but beforehand, she needed to say something. She said, "Marilyn, I will pray for you, but I had been wanting to talk to you about your driving (code for I have been praying for you about your driving). You have to consider the way you are driving and begin to change that... " She went on to say some other things, but frankly, she lost me on "wanting to talk to you about your driving." I remember getting very mad and thinking that I didn't ask her to tell me about my driving, but rather, she just needed to pray this fine away. When she finished and it was time to pray, I was so offended and full of pride that I told her that I had changed my mind; I didn't feel up to praying after all. I'm absolutely sure that it was the Holy Spirit who led me to this friend to have her to pray for me, but not to pray away the consequences of my actions. Instead, He wanted to use her to correct my thinking and conduct.

When I arrived home, I found that I could not escape the conviction of the Holy Ghost. I had to face the truth; my driving was out of control. My willingness to face this fact opened the door for me to see other things I had to face about myself that God wanted to correct such as pride, mismanagement of money and mismanagement of time. Humility goes a long way with the Spirit; He gives grace to the humble. He gave me the grace to pick up my phone, call my mentor, apologize and admit that I was wrong.

During this period of my life, I was getting acquainted with the convicting power of the Holy Ghost. I found that the Holy

Spirit was teaching me obedience and holiness through the conviction I felt at certain times and that my conscience was bearing witness to the Holy Spirit. Conviction opens the door for repentance, and repentance opens the door for change. Change is something else I learned about discipleship.

Jesus said in John 14:15, "If ye love me, keep my commandments." In this passage, Jesus challenges the disciples to show their love for Him by keeping His commandments. I love that after having done so, He brings our attention to the "Comforter" in the very next verse, saying, "And I will pray the Father, and he shall give you another Comforter that he may abide with you for ever." In essence, Jesus was reassuring us that the "Comforter" who brings the love of the Father into our hearts would be there with us to help us prove our love to God through the keeping of His commandments.

In His earthly life, Jesus pleased the Father and was obedient unto death. He was compassionate towards the poor and hurting, plus, He walked in love and fulfilled His purpose in life. Jesus is the ultimate example of godly living. The Bible teaches us that Jesus is the actual expressed image of the invisible God (see Colossians 1:15). When we see Jesus, we see God. The Spirit of God now living in me was revealing Christ to me and compelled me to want to please the Father as Jesus did. By now, I realized that making the decision to follow Christ was a lifestyle choice in which I would become more sanctified (holy) over a period of time. God is holy, and because He is holy, we must become holy in our thinking, our moral character and ultimately, our lifestyles.

One way to look at this is that the Holy Spirit would conform me to the image of Jesus Christ over the course of my life (see Romans 8:29). II Corinthians 3:18 confirms this, "But we all, with unveiled face, beholding as in a mirror the glory of the Lord, are being transformed into the same image from glory to glory, just as by the Spirit of the Lord." Disciples are "changed" into the image of Jesus Christ! The Holy Spirit had begun the process of my transformation, and I held to the promise that He would most certainly complete the work He had begun in me!

Chapter Seven

Study: Fellowship: Mentorship

"Go ye therefore, and teach all nations, baptizing them in the name of the Father, and of the Son, and of the Holy Ghost: Teaching them to observe all things whatsoever I have commanded you: and, lo, I am with you always, even unto the end of the world. Amen."
Matthew 28:19-20

In Matthew 28:19, Jesus gave instruction to His disciples saying, "Go ye therefore, and teach all nations, baptizing them in the name of the Father, and of the Son, and of the Holy Ghost..." In order to gain a more significant understanding of this commandment from Jesus, let's look at two key words contained within this passage of scripture using the *Strong's Concordance* definitions: "baptizing" and "name." The Greek word for "baptizing" is "baptizō" and it simply means to fully submerge or immerse into something. For example, one could be "baptizō" into water, the Holy Spirit or like in the present scripture, "baptizing in the name..." The Greek word for "name" is "o'-no-mä"and the *Strong's Concordance* gives the following description of how it is biblically used: "the name is used for everything which the name covers, everything the thought or feeling of which is aroused in the mind by mentioning, hearing, remembering, the name, i.e. for one's rank, authority, interests, pleasure, command, excellences, deeds etc." In other words, when Jesus said, "baptizing in the name of the Father, and of the Son, and of the Holy Ghost...," He was pretty much saying to fully submerge people in the character, authority, command etc. of the Godhead. This is why He said, "Go ye therefore and teach..."

A disciple of Christ is expected to grow in such a way that he or she is able to teach others what they have learned. We are being conformed to the image of Christ, and not just in name, but in becoming the character, thought, and moral deed of God, the Father, Son, and Holy Spirit.

God intends for our growth to be permanent so that He may be glorified to others through His disciples. I came across the following explanation of the word "baptizo", and it gives us a great picture of what being fully submerged in God's character should be: "The clearest example that shows the meaning of baptizo is a text from the Greek poet and physician Nicander, who lived about 200 B.C. It is a recipe for making pickles and is helpful because it uses both words. Nicander says that in order to make a pickle, the vegetable should first be 'dipped' (baptô) into boiling water and then 'baptized' (baptizô) in the vinegar solution. Both verbs concern the immersing of vegetables in a solution. But the first is temporary. The second, the act of baptizing the vegetable, produces a permanent change" (Ref: *The Blue Letter Bible website*).

In order for a disciple to become permanently changed and equipped to share the things of God to others, that disciple must become teachable. The Word says in II Timothy 2:15, "Study to shew thyself approved unto God, a workman that needeth not to be ashamed, rightly dividing the word of truth." We must have godly examples because I Corinthians 15:33 teaches us that "evil communications corrupt good manners." We must have some form of accountability in our lives because Proverbs 27:17 points out that, "As iron sharpens iron, so a man sharpens the countenance of his friend." Ecclesiastes 4:9-10 says, "Two are better than one, Because they have a good reward for their labor. For if they fall, one will lift up his companion. But woe to him who is alone when he falls, For he has no one to help him up."

The Holy Spirit knew the plan of God for my life and He also knew what I needed in order to be prepared for where God was taking me. He divinely ordered my steps away from ungodly relationships to godly ones.

By now, I had a few wonderful friends in my life who served as godly examples to me. They themselves were disciples of Christ. Paul said in I Corinthians 11:1 (AMP), "Pattern yourselves after me [follow my example], as I imitate and follow Christ (the Messiah)." So this was what I was doing. Following women of God who had more experience in the Christian walk than I did. These women had such a love for God. What better way to grow in the grace of God and in my walk with Christ than to hang out with people who also desired to grow and give devotion to Christ.

Some of the things that I loved most about them was their enthusiasm and the sense of duty they had in sharing the things of God with me. For example, it was within these newly formed relationships that I began to see God, the Father as my "Papa or Daddy." At first, this was peculiar to me because up until that point in my life, I didn't know that there was such a relationship that one could have with God. Sure, when I was growing up in the church, I knew Him as the Father in heaven, but it was pretty much a formality and not a real relationship like Father and daughter. Besides, I didn't really know what such a relationship was since I didn't grow up with my father around. These women repeatedly referred to God as "Daddy" and I loved it. Galatians 4:6 uses the Greek word "Abba" which, to some scholars, implies a more intimate and informal relationship. It is more like saying "daddy" than saying "father." It reads, "And because ye are sons, God hath sent forth the Spirit of his Son into your hearts, crying, Abba, Father." As I grew in fellowship with these few women, I also grew in an intimate fellowship with the Father, my "Papa, Daddy."

To some degree, I already knew Him to be a Father in the sense of provider and protector, so as I would hear the testimonies of how "Daddy" had provided much needed headshots, a full tank of gas for the week, a new outfit and even a new car, I was encouraged. However, I came to understand a father's more intimate role to his child over time, as we continued to fellowship with one another.

At times, we would pile up into one of our cars to head off to an open casting call for a theatrical play, some industry seminar or for some special event. Always, the conversations would be God-centered as His "daughters" would brag about what "Daddy" was doing in their lives. I would hear sweet stories of the affectionate "Daddy" who allowed His daughter to "climb up into His lap," so to speak, and cry when she was going through a hard time. There, in "His lap of prayer," she would receive the loving counsel and affirmation needed in a way that only a daddy could give his daughter. Other stories would give accounts of how "Daddy" had given discipline and correction when it was most needed. This encouraged me to get to know Him as "Daddy" in my own intimate way and I did.

A key instance was "Daddy's" response to me one day when I was a bit thoughtful concerning my past childhood. I hadn't realized that I was carrying so much disappointment in my heart, but it was a good day to become aware of it. On this particular day, I was complaining to Him about the fact that throughout my childhood, my earthly father wasn't around, so I had missed out on knowing how it feels to be loved, protected, accepted and celebrated unconditionally. I pointed out that I hadn't remembered him ever being at one of the few birthday parties I had or to any of the track meets and basketball games that I had competed in. "Where was he when I needed him to rescue me from molestation and rape and from being bullied into fighting girls by much older boys?," I asked.

My thoughts had to do mainly with high school years when I needed correction or guidance on how to conduct myself in certain matters that are important to a teenage girl such as boys and best friends. I pointed out that my earthly father wasn't around when my sister and I both were chosen to be on the homecoming queen's court during our high school football season, instead, it was our uncles who had escorted us onto the football field as our names were called. I just began to pour out my heart to God and I was pouring it out pretty heavily and digging deep into my emotions.

I was on a roll and as I was gaining some ground on my case against my earthly father, I heard this still small voice calmly and lovingly say, "I was there." Just as I was about to point out that my earthly father hadn't been there to affirm me when I received any of the many awards of merit for my achievements as an athlete and scholar, my "Papa, Daddy" dried my tears with just a few words.

My immediate response was not the obvious question most women would ask, which is, "Why didn't you do something?" Instead, a sense of relief came over me and I was happy that I'd made it through. God, my "Papa, Daddy" had allowed me to "climb up into His lap," and not just so I could wallow in my woes and have a self-pity party because there is always a greater purpose with God. I was seeking comfort and affirmation and "Daddy" was after deliverance. With those few words, "I was there," came a level of comfort I had not yet experienced and it made everything alright for that moment of despair. Somehow, I knew that God, the Father was offering me something much more than a moment of peace, but He was offering me a permanent resolution.

At just the right moment, He interrupted my stream of thoughts, downloaded revelation knowledge into my heart to redirect my thoughts and changed my perspective. I went from the "woe is me" mentality to the "blessed am I" mentality. I'm in no way minimizing what I went through in my childhood, after all, the pain was real, the damage was done and I had suffered through it. From my childhood mentality, I had been rejected, abandoned, and consequently, rendered inferior to others because I had no father or mother to look to while growing up. The door to self-doubt, low self-esteem and self-worth had been opened for the enemy to run freely through my emotional life and self-perception.

However, in this crucial moment, revelation knowledge came to me making me aware of who "Abba, Father" is to me on a personal level. Psalm 27:10 reads, "When my father and my mother forsake me, then the LORD will take me up." I was presented with a solution. Either I could continue to wallow in my woes or I could choose to put my hand in my Abba Father's hand and allow Him to bring me out of it and elevate my thinking.

The answer was easy because as I stated previously, God can say a whole lot in just a few words. Those few words, "I was there," meant to me that He had been listening to me and He cared about me. When He answered, "I was there," His response confirmed what I'd believed and claimed all along: that my earthly father had not been there for me. In validating my claim, my pain, suffering and loss were validated. I opted for the permanent solution because, in those few words, I knew that He could be trusted. In those few words, "I was there," I heard my Abba Father saying, "I know how you feel," "I know where you are broken" and, most importantly, "I know how to fix you."

Those few words said to me that if I would just take my Daddy's hand and was willing to move forward, I would begin to take on His perspective. I understood that my perspective, though it was a truth, was inconclusive as far as my Daddy was concerned. My perspective was one-sided, which meant, in the most harmless way, that it was selfish and self-centered. There were sides to my earthly father's story that I needed to understand in order to get a truthful perspective. If I was willing, my "Papa, Daddy" would take me by the hand to a place of healing and forgiveness. When the Lord said, "I was there," I understood that the journey to healing would not be an easy one, but He would hold my hand along the way.

I also heard in those words that God, the Father knew me before He assigned my earthly father to me and conceived me in my mother's womb. He knew the set of circumstances that I would face in my life. Psalm 139:13 and 16 confirm this. It reads, "You alone created my inner being. You knitted me together inside my mother." And "Your eyes saw me when I was still an unborn child. Every day of my life was recorded in your book before one of them had taken place." I heard in those words, "I was there" that, even though you were robbed of an intimate relationship with your father, mistreated, abused and abandoned, you are still fearfully and wonderfully made. Regardless of what the enemy did to harm you, I am more than able to turn it around for your good."

Somehow, without Him having to say it, I knew that the good that He wanted to do in me would call for a permanent change. I was that "pickle" that would be fully baptized and not just dipped. It was part of the journey to becoming a disciple well able to disciple others. Change came when I started looking at Jesus through the Word, the eyes of the Holy Spirit and through seeing Him in others.

Whatever work the Holy Spirit was doing in me, I could see it in these special few women as well. 1 John 1:3 declares, "What we have seen and heard we proclaim to you also, so that you too may have fellowship with us; and indeed our fellowship is with the Father, and with His Son Jesus Christ." God delights in our loving fellowship with one another. He holds great value in it as well. I have grown to understand the importance of letting go of worldly friends when I think about the great benefit of seeing Jesus in others.

If I wasn't willing to let go of certain people, the work that the Holy Spirit was doing in me on a daily basis would have been hindered. The old Marilyn was gone; I was a new creation in Christ Jesus. The old ways, thoughts, and beliefs were slowly passing away and the new Marilyn with her godly beliefs, patterns of thinking and ways were coming forth. Those who knew the old Marilyn on an intimate basis would have undone the work of God during my infant stage of Christianity because evil communications corrupt good manners. Whoever you spend time with and hang out with, you begin to look like, talk like and act like, after all, "birds of a feather do flock together." He was taking away bad habits, changing my thinking and convicting me in my conduct. My godly friends were right there setting the example and holding me accountable.

There was one woman in particular that I was beginning to spend a great deal of time with. In just about a week after having been delivered from those demons, I found myself over my new friend's house and she would become my mentor. At that time, I was still up for the role in the independent film and she was supposed to help me get ready for the meeting with the director, or so I thought.

The Holy Spirit had another plan. I spent the better part of the afternoon at her house and the script for the movie did not come up one time. From the time I arrived until I left about four or five hours later, the subject had been the Word of God. I was captivated by the wonders of the gospel from the time she opened her mouth and began to share as the Holy Spirit led her. She had a way of drawing you in when it came to expounding on the Word of God too. During subsequent visits, as a way of illustrating certain truths, she used her favorite cartoon characters and episodes, personalities of family members (young and old alike) and anything or anyone else that came to mind to make understanding the gospel easier.

On one particular visit, she leaped to her feet like a super hero and, while standing in the middle of the living room where we sat, began to recite Ephesians 6:13-17. This was the scripture about putting on the full armor of God. As she called out the pieces of armor, she would dramatically gesture to the corresponding body parts where the Roman soldiers would wear them. I felt like a kid at the children's theater matinee, and in my heart, I was giving her a standing ovation, silently screaming, "Encore, encore!" I wanted more. I was like a sponge soaking it all in; I did not want her to stop talking. I know it sounds a little juvenile and elementary, but the Holy Spirit knew exactly what I needed. I Peter 2:2 reads, "As newborn babes, desire the sincere milk of the word, that ye may grow thereby." I was a newborn babe with a huge appetite for my spiritual food; I couldn't get enough of the Word. My spiritual eyes and ears were wide open and from that very first encounter, I would begin to learn about the very foundations of Christian living from her.

She became one of the tools the Holy Spirit would use to disciple me. She had knowledge and enthusiasm. It was obvious that she was someone who spent time both reading and studying the Word of God. And her knowledge of the Bible inspired me to want to read and study the Bible for myself. I took her up on her offer to go online and order everything I would need to do so. It was sort of a starter kit on studying the gospel. She ordered a study Bible, the Strong's Exhaustive Concordance, the Vine's Complete Expository Dictionary, Jamieson, Fausset & Brown's Commentary on the whole Bible, and a few other books she thought I should read. I came to find out later that this was a service she offered to many who she encountered with a hunger for the deeper things of God.

I was so grateful for her services that I gave her far more money than what I owed. I only share this because it's a testimony of how the Holy Spirit was dealing with me. He had influenced me to invest in my spiritual life. Just as I would invest in my acting career, my personal appearance and other things in life that were important to me, so I did with the things of God.

I was willing to invest my time into learning how to use my new tools as well. I gathered a few other ladies together and asked my friend to host a few in-home Bible lessons on how to study the Bible. After much prayer, she agreed to do so. The Lord had confirmed to her saying, "Teach them how to fish." He told her that it would be just a few lessons because as the saying goes, "Give a man a fish and he'll eat for a day, but teach him how to fish and he'll eat for a lifetime." In the book of John, Jesus told His disciples to keep His commandments. In order to keep His commandments, we must know His commands. The Holy Spirit wasn't interested in feeding me just for the moment, but more in bringing me into a lifelong relationship with the Word of God. He would teach me to stand up and become accountable for knowing what God's Word says and for keeping it.

Our first assignment was to look up the word "salvation" in the *Strong's Concordance*. We were instructed to read and then write down all the scripture references listed next to this word, both in the Hebrew (Old Testament) and the Greek (New Testament). It was a tedious assignment, but the outcome had a profound effect on the way in which I would read and study the Word from then on.

Beforehand, my understanding of our English word "salvation" was simply that Jesus, through dying on the cross, provided forgiveness of my past sins and therefore, I have eternal life. During my study time, I came to understand that salvation is so much more than going to heaven when I die. In looking at the definition, I came across such words and phrases as: rescue, deliverance, help, preserve prosperity, welfare, defense, saving health, to be made whole, heal, do well and to be free. In my commentator, I would come across such phrases as: delivered from harm's way, recover from loss and to slacken the hold of the enemy.

Pretty much, in one day, my basic understanding of what I had in salvation went from being forgiven of my sins in order to go to heaven when I die to including a much broader perspective. I learned that my salvation benefits also included the promise of being healed from bodily infirmities, brokenness of mind and all emotional strongholds. On the day of my salvation, God made me whole in soul, spirit and body and this wholeness accounted for the peace that I was feeling. That peace became something much more than a feeling, it became something concrete and tangible. That peace was the proof of my restored relationship with God and this knowledge gave me boldness in approaching Him in prayer.

I came to understand that this peace also referred to prosperity, and prosperity meant more than mere financial gain. I could expect a prosperous spiritual life because the Word of God said so. I came across such scriptures like 3 John 1:3, "Beloved, I wish above all things that thou mayest prosper and be in health, even as thy soul prospereth." I had been rescued from harm's way and I began to see God as my defender instead of the punisher. Jesus said that He came to give life more abundantly (see John 10:10). Now that I'm saved, I'm living the abundant life.

How appropriate for God to choose the topic of "salvation" as my first study assignment. As a disciple, this is where it all begins: with our salvation. With this new understanding, what I gained was a far cry from the religious perspective that limited my knowledge of who God is and what I have in Him. It was a profound teaching to me and it made the difference in me becoming more rooted in the faith, whereas in my previous Christian walk, I had been in and out of the church like it had revolving doors. Now, I was empowered to develop a more meaningful and loving relationship with Christ. Because I was becoming equipped to look deeper in the written commandments of God, He was drawing me deeper; deeper in His love, deeper in the Word, deeper in worship and deeper in my knowledge of the fullness of Him. Certainly, God had a plan.

This new way of reading and studying the Bible would become a permanent discipline in my personal devotional life. I had begun to "fish." After a few classes, I would go on to study other subjects such as righteousness, sanctification and the blood of Jesus in the same manner in which I had learned. I would bring this discipline into my prayer time as well. Oftentimes, I would set aside time for prayer, but partway into my prayer time, I'd get caught up in studying a particular scripture. It was paying off too. By this time, I was learning to use scriptures in prayer, so now, even my prayer life was being revolutionized by my new discipline of study. My new friend was right there with me too. By this time, I had gotten it; she had been divinely chosen by God to mentor me, and now, she was being divinely used to help birth in me a love and respect for prayer.

At the time, I didn't know that God called me to be an intercessor. The gift of prayer was on me so strong that I don't ever remember not knowing how to pray. It's kind of like how I first began to swim as a child. I never knew I couldn't swim, so when the first opportunity presented itself, I just dove right in and began to swim. I operated in the gift of warfare prophetic prayers in the same way. I just dove right in.

God had used a few people to activate it and to train me in it. There were two on the TBN channel that I found: Creflo Dollar and Joyce Meyer. Beginning from about four o'clock in the morning until about six o'clock in the morning, for a period of about four weeks, each would come right after the other teaching on prayer. Morning after morning, one would pick up where the other left off. It seemed to me that they had a conspiracy going and that was to tag team and teach Marilyn Love some principles on prayer.

Then there was my mentor. She was the practical example of everything I was learning from the two on the Christian network. During the course of our first year, we spent plenty of time together, whether it was going to church services together, having lunch or dinner or just hanging out and running errands together. I loved to hang out with her because I always knew what to expect, which was a few hours of Christ-centered conversations well spent.

On many of these excursions, she would invite me into one of her prayer closets: her car. Like clockwork, from the time I would get into her car and before we would reach our destination, we would have prayed for numerous people. These people included prostitutes on the sidewalk, people walking, accidents on the highway, people getting pulled over by the police and even ourselves. Talk about drive-by shootings; the gangs didn't have anything on us. We did some drive-by praying. I suspect a lot of unsuspecting people benefited from our warfare prayers. God was teaching me how to have compassion for others just as Jesus had compassion for those who came to Him, but more than that, He was teaching me the discipline of effective warfare intercession.

During these times together, we were not praying pretty little prayers that sounded nice to sweet Jesus, but we commenced to binding the power of the prince of the air in our neighborhoods and wherever we drove. We would discern what demons were at work and what strongholds were in effect as we left one neighborhood and entered the next. My friend would always take the lead to set a good sound precedence for our standing in our rightful place of authority. She would proclaim the name of Jesus, the blood of Jesus and would quote scripture after scripture throughout our time of prayer. She would remind me of our power through agreement, and the principles of disallowing and permitting what is already done in heaven based on Matthew 18:18-19. As we bound the powers and principalities, the rulers of the darkness of the world and the spiritual wickedness in heavenly places, we would spend time also releasing the power of God in the neighborhoods.

We would speak the solution: healing and deliverance over the prostitutes, rather than the problem. According to scripture, we would command the angels who were sent to serve those who were "heirs of salvation" to war on our behalf, hearkening to the one voicing the Word of God (see Hebrews 1:14, Psalm 103:20). We would remind God that He said He was looking for a man to stand in the gap as we presented ourselves in prayer for the lost. We would often petition God for salvation and deliverance to come upon the homes that we passed by. If we came upon an accident, we could have been accused by others of "rubber necking," but in truth, we were stretching our hands forth to rebuke the spirit of death. We were sowing our prayers into the kingdom of God. The Word says to lay up treasures in heaven. Hopefully, when I get to heaven, I'll get to meet some of those prostitutes, gang members and sickly folk we prayed for during those times.

I found that the gift of prophetic prayer was in operation, both in my friend's car and in my home as well. I would often spend hours of my prayer time decreeing the Word of God over my own life as the Spirit gave me utterance. It was there in my prayer closet that I began to "call those things that were not as though they were" (see Romans 4:16-18). As I spent time praying in my heavenly language, the Holy Spirit would begin to impress upon my heart what to rebuke, what to repent of, what to denounce and what scriptural truths to stand on for my life. The anointing would fall upon me for faith enough to believe that I was receiving what I was praying for even while I was praying. The Holy Spirit was training me to be a "mountain mover" through my prayers as I began to speak with authority over the demons of lust, lack and sickness, commanding them to be removed (see Mark 11:23). I began to lead myself through deliverance to where I would cough and spit confirming that something was being uprooted. I took authority over any family curses I knew of that could have been operating illegally in my life. I would tell Satan that I knew my rights; I knew that Christ had become a curse for me so I no longer had to live under any curses (see Galatians 3:13). After having spoken to the Devil in this way, I would rise up with such an anointing to declare my freedom from the blood line curse of the addiction to drugs and alcohol, depression and schizophrenia. Jesus said that He gave us authority to tread on serpents and scorpions, and over all the power of the enemy (see Luke 10:19), and this was just what I was doing. I was trampling the necks of the enemies of my past, present and future.

The Holy Spirit was teaching me to wield His weapon: the Word of God against the enemy. Oftentimes, I felt like fire was coming out of my own mouth as I stood my ground, decreeing the Word of God. In these times especially, there was no need for me to read a scripture to confess or read a prayer that I had written; the prayer would just come forth like water pouring out of an overturned bottle.

I could always tell when I had entered into another realm because I would begin to see what I hadn't seen before by revelation and visions. I was like Ezekiel who by the hand of the Lord was carried out into the spiritual realm and shown the valley of dry bones. There, God also gave him a command to prophesy upon the bones, telling the bones to "hear the Word of God" as he began to prophesy (see Ezekiel 37). I too began to prophesy as I was shown what strongholds and hindrances the devil had set in my life.

Not just for myself either, God would use me during these times to pray prophetic prayers for family members. There would be plenty of mornings that if I had to leave before I was released, my prayer closet would be extended to my car just as I had done with my mentor. On one particular morning, in route to an early appointment, I continued praying for my family members. I had a breakthrough where there was a sudden outpour of the gift of faith upon me, in me and through me. This faith was so real to me that even if I wanted to doubt what was coming out of my mouth, I couldn't. Shortly afterwards, I began to hear from family members I hadn't talked to in years. They shared wonderful testimonies of how they and other family members were back in the church and serving God. I'm sure they had also been benefiting from the prayers of our grandparents, uncles and aunts just as I had, but I knew that I was also a co-laborer with God in intercessory prayer concerning my family. I was giving back, as many of my family members do through prayer to this day.

This was the time in my life when I found out that one can experience exciting and powerful times of prayer if they are willing to sacrifice time and their flesh to God for His purposes. Romans 12:1 declares, "I beseech you therefore, brethren, by the mercies of God, that ye present your bodies a living sacrifice, holy, acceptable unto God, which is your reasonable service." Christ said, the spirit is willing, but it's the flesh that is weak. As I became willing and presented myself to God, the Holy Spirit would do the rest; He would use my body to labor in prayer. I was learning that offering my body to God wasn't just about abstaining from premarital sex, but allowing the Holy Spirit to do His work through me, as confirmed in I Corinthians 6:19-20: "What? Know ye not that your body is the temple of the Holy Ghost which is in you, which ye have of God, and ye are not your own? For ye are bought with a price: therefore glorify God in your body, and in your spirit, which are God's." The Holy Spirit was glorifying God through me. There were other areas of reasonable service to God that I would be initiated into during this time in my walk with Christ. One such service was evangelism.

On some of those occasions when we were out together, my friend and mentor would witness to others at stores and other public places. I remember the very first time she did this. We were at a busy lighting store because she was in the market for a new chandelier for her home. We were browsing through the store when she noticed a man standing in the middle of the aisle that we had just turned onto. After a few minutes, she struck up a friendly conversation with him. Before I knew it, she was leading him to Christ, right there in the middle of the store. With tears coming from his eyes, he had accepted Christ into his life and began to share how he had once known Him. What's ironic is that the store we were in sold all sorts of lights, but we were the brightest lights shining in that moment. Paul declared in Romans 1:16, "For I am not ashamed of the gospel of Christ: for it is the power of God unto salvation to every one that believeth..." My mentor definitely was not ashamed of the gospel, and neither was I.

I had learned through the altar workers class how to lead someone to Christ and had seen good success from serving in that capacity from within the church building. Before long, I realized that God was expecting me to carry the gospel outside of the church building and I had learned through these experiences with my mentor that there was a need for altar workers anywhere and everywhere; the altar is portable. It can go with you in the grocery stores, busy restaurants and on television sets. I quickly fell into the habit of being on the alert for a "Christ moment" anytime I went anywhere. I have to admit that sometimes it was a little overdone or, better yet, there were some cases when it was well overdone, but this was the benefit of having someone in my life who would train me, serve as a godly example to me and hold me accountable to what I was learning.

More of my ministry gifts were being activated as I was becoming more and more faithful to what I was learning. I had begun to operate in the prophetic. It was crucial to my growth to have an accountability partner because with God, character is always first. It's a dangerous place to operate in ministry gifts with no accountability. By doing so, one can cause great harm, both to oneself and to others. Paul taught about the character of love being the greatest gift we can have in I Corinthians 13:1-3 (NKJV). It reads, "Though I speak with the tongues of men and of angels, but have not love, I have become sounding brass or a clanging cymbal. And though I have the gift of prophecy, and understand all mysteries and all knowledge, and though I have all faith, so that I could remove mountains, but have not love, I am nothing." I didn't want to end up as nothing. Paul went on in verses 4-7 to explain what a healthy minister looked like in their love walk. He said, "Love suffers long and is kind; love does not envy; love does not parade itself, is not puffed up; does not behave rudely, does not seek its own, is not provoked, thinks no evil; does not rejoice in iniquity, but rejoices in the truth; bears all things, believes all things, hopes all things, endures all things." Yes, I needed an accountability partner and was happy to have a few.

Chapter Eight

<u>My Old Self: Renewed Mind: A New Woman</u>

"That ye put off concerning the former conversation the old man, which is corrupt according to the deceitful lusts; and be renewed in the spirit of your mind; and that ye put on the new man, which after God is created in righteousness and true holiness."
Ephesians 4:22-24

Attending church at least twice weekly had become a part of my new lifestyle as well. It was a choice that I gladly welcomed. I looked forward to being in the presence of the Lord and hearing the Word of God. I considered it a privilege to attend a church where the Word of God was being preached and taught in a way that provoked change in my mindset and lifestyle. However, what really made a big difference in my spiritual growth as a disciple was that as I "heard" the truth from the preaching of the Word, I had now become equipped to "see" the truth for myself in the Word of God as I studied it.

I would use my new study tools and skills to study what I was hearing and there was great benefit in this. In the fourth chapter of Mark, Jesus spoke in a parable about the different conditions of the heart where the Word of God is sown. Afterwards, He warned that we should give heed to what we hear because the closer we listen and the more thought we give to what we hear, the more understanding we would receive. And from that understanding, even more understanding would be given (see Mark 4:24). Just as God had great purposes in my study of the word "salvation" as my first word study assignment, He would use the first message series that I would hear and study to make an impression upon me, and surely, the first impression was a lasting one.

The title of the teaching series my pastor started shortly after I joined the church was, "What's Up with Your Old Man?!" This was an in-depth teaching on the necessity of having the mind renewed and would become the "theme song" of my life for the next several years. This message helped me to better understand who I was in Christ, what God expected of me and what I needed to do in order to grow in Christ. It was the next logical step after salvation, which I hadn't known before. It answered the questions that every new Christian should ask, "Now that I'm saved, now what? What's next?"

For me, it was the catalyst that brought about deep emotional healing and deliverance from past issues. It brought recovery from bad thinking habits, belief systems and perceptions that didn't serve me well, and it brought correction to character flaws and faults I didn't even know I had. Paul said in I Corinthians 13:11, "When I was a child, I spake as a child, I understood as a child, I thought as a child: but when I became a man, I put away childish things." This message also proved to be pivotal to my radical spiritual growth as I became more of a woman of God and less of a child of the Devil, which was my pre-converted state.

The foundational scripture passage used for this in-depth teaching was from Ephesians 4:22-24, "That ye put off concerning the former conversation the old man, which is corrupt according to the deceitful lusts; and be renewed in the spirit of your mind; and that ye put on the new man, which after God is created in righteousness and true holiness."

I came to understand that the worldly and defeated lifestyle I had been living as a Christian was due largely in part to the fact that I had been alienated from the life of God. Therefore, I was in spiritual darkness with no moral understanding or godly wisdom. This was the consequence of sin, which those without Christ suffer. Before I was born again, I was spiritually dead. This fact was important to understand because knowing it emphasized the need to have my mind recovered from my old life and the old me.

Being in moral darkness is a human condition in which the first man Adam brought upon all through his one act of rebellion (see Romans 5:12). Originally, Adam was created in the image of God, so he was in perfect harmony with God: spirit, soul and body. Genesis 1:26-27 reads, "And God said, Let us make man in Our image, after Our likeness: So God created man in His own image, in the image of God created He him; male and female created He them." The Hebrew word used for God in these passages is "Elohim." It's a plural word used for one of the names of God referred to as God the Father, God the Son and God the Holy Spirit. These are the Godhead which Romans 1:20 speaks of, and it reads, "For the invisible things of Him from the creation of the world are clearly seen, being understood by the things that are made, **even His eternal power and Godhead**; so that they are without excuse."

Just as the Godhead is three, so Adam was created with three parts known as the tripartite Man, in the form of a body, soul and spirit. We can see how God accomplished this when we read Genesis 2:7, "And the LORD God formed man of the dust of the ground, and breathed into his nostrils the breath of life; and man became a living soul." Clearly from this scripture, we can see that Adam became a living soul when God breathed His breath (Ruach) into Adam's spirit. His breath in this passage, implies His Spirit. *Wikipedia,* the free encyclopedia, gives an explanation of the word "Ruach." We know that it was Adam's spirit where God's breath or Spirit rested in Adam because Proverbs 20:27 teaches us that the human spirit is the lamp that the LORD uses to shine His light in one's inmost being. I Thessalonians 5:23 also confirms that we are three parts, "And the very God of peace sanctify you wholly; and I pray God your whole spirit and soul and body be preserved blameless unto the coming of our Lord Jesus Christ."

These prove that man is three parts; we have a soul, we have a spirit and we live in a body. Our body (the flesh) houses our soul and spirit. Our soul is made up of the heart (to feel, emotions), the mind (to think; it is our intellect) and the will (our decision maker). Our spirit is our intuitive self; it's how we commune with God. So, we can see that Adam was in perfect harmony with God since he was created in His image and had His Spirit within him. He not only had God in the Garden of Eden with him, he also had God living in him.

However, God cannot dwell where sin is. Genesis 2:17 tells us that Adam was given a commandment from God, and it reads, "But of the tree of the knowledge of good and evil, thou shalt not eat of it: for in the day that thou eatest thereof thou shalt surely die." When Adam disobeyed his Master's commandment by eating of the fruit of that tree, he died spiritually. Consequently, his spirit, where he communed with God, no longer had access to the light of life; he was now in utter darkness. He was left without his moral compass. He did not experience physical death right away, even though his eyes were immediately opened and he felt the guilt and shame associated with sin, rebellion and death.

Because of that transgression, the Bible records the condition of man as a result of the first man, Adam's sin. Genesis 6:5-6, "And GOD saw that the wickedness of man was great in the earth, and that every imagination of the thoughts of his heart was only evil continually." Adam's sin separated him from God. Since God communed with Adam through Adam's spirit, Adam was rendered spiritually dead. He was now a living soul with a spirit but without a spiritual connection to God; he was separated from divine wisdom. Without access to God's wisdom, we are left up to our own wicked and vain thoughts, and we will use our soul, our own emotions, intellect, and will as our compasses in life. We have a heart and mind (emotional and intellectual) -- a soul condition (our own will) -- that does not want to please God.

Ephesians 4:17-19 (NLT) describes, to some degree, my condition before having been born again. This is the apostle Paul talking to Christians. It reads, "With the Lord's authority I say this: Live no longer as the Gentiles do, for they are hopelessly confused. Their minds are full of darkness; they wander far from the life God gives because they have closed their minds and hardened their hearts against him. They have no sense of shame. They live for lustful pleasure and eagerly practice every kind of impurity."

I know in my life, I had been doing what seemed right to me, but even in my purest thoughts and actions, I had been far from God because I was without Christ. Jeremiah 17:9 declares, "The heart is deceitful above all things, and desperately wicked: who can know it?" The heart is the inner man, mind of our soul; it is not the spirit or the innermost man where God abides. The condition of a man's heart or soul really dictates the moral character of that man. Consider the following passage of scripture (Matthew 15:17-20) where Christ teaches this truth, "Do not ye yet understand, that whatsoever entereth in at the mouth goeth into the belly, and is cast out into the draught? But those things which proceed out of the mouth come forth from the heart; and they defile the man. For out of the heart proceeds evil thoughts, murders, adulteries, fornications, thefts, false witness, blasphemies: These are the things which defile a man: but to eat with unwashen hands defileth not a man." In this passage, Christ gave us a list of the things that spring forth from our hearts to defile us.

In Matthew 5:27-28, Christ teaches the following, "You have heard that it was said to those of old, 'You shall not commit adultery. But I say to you that whoever looks at a woman to lust for her has already committed adultery with her in his heart." Thoughts give birth to actions. A man who has gone through with the act of adultery has actually sinned when the very thought came to him from within his heart. Again, it's a condition of the pre-converted state because Christ said that it's not what goes into a man that defiles him; it's what comes forth from the heart. Notice that in the present scripture, Christ actually recites from the book of the law, the seventh commandment listed in Exodus, chapter 20. God told us that if a man lives by the law, he will have to keep the whole law. Breaking one would bring eternal death. Galatians 3:10 reads, "For all who rely on the works of the law are under a curse, as it is written: 'Cursed is everyone who does not continue to do everything written in the Book of the Law.'" According to Christ's teaching, if we are under the ten commandments, it's safe to say that we are condemned by the condition of our hearts and not by our actions.

Sadly, no one could keep the law. Our hope was pretty bleak, but God had a plan in the form of Christ our Savior. Galatians 3:13-14 (AMP) gives us hope, "Christ purchased our freedom and redeemed us from the curse of the law and its condemnation by becoming a curse for us—for it is written, 'Cursed is everyone who hangs [crucified] on a tree (cross)'— in order that in Christ Jesus the blessing of Abraham might also come to the Gentiles, so that we would all receive [the realization of] the promise of the [Holy] Spirit through faith." Because of the finished work of the cross, we received the Spirit of God back into our spirits, thereby giving us communion with God and access to His wisdom again.

Understanding the effect my pre-converted state had on my mind convinced me that I indeed needed to subject my mind to the will of God. The more I studied this teaching, the more I pondered my own thinking patterns. I began to give thought to what I was thinking about on a daily basis, and I did this on purpose. More and more, I began to see how my negative thoughts, perceptions, and beliefs were based on experiences in my childhood. There were some pretty painful moments I lived through and like a video recorder, my mind captured those moments. It pretty much captured every detail down to the person(s) involvement, what they did, how it was done and how it made me feel emotionally at the time.

I even had a record of what I thought were my inadequate reactions to some of those moments. I gave myself an opportunity to take part in the "blame game" that I secretly played in my heart.

The light from the Word of God that I was studying was beginning to shine intensely on my thinking patterns and belief systems, which both had to do with my perceptions of myself. I came to realize that these negative thoughts and beliefs directly affected my self -esteem and self-worth and that my own perceptions of myself directly affected my actions. Proverbs 23:7 says, "For as he thinketh in his heart, so is he..." In other words, "As a man thinks, so is his behavior." If I had feelings, beliefs and thoughts of failure and defeat, I would live a life of failure and defeat. My eyes were wide open and I was ready for change.

The answer was in putting on the new man. Thank God that through our salvation, having received the Spirit of Christ, we have been given the mind of Christ (see I Corinthians 2:16). Afterwards, we just need to commence to subjecting our souls (mind, will and emotions) to the mind of Christ. I was convinced that my paradigm of thinking needed an overhaul and the solution was in putting on the mind of Christ, His thoughts and will. But before that could happen, I would need to deal with my "old man."

In Ephesians 4:22-24, Paul emphasizes the need for change. He says, we must "...put on the new man, which after God is righteousness and true holiness." His audience was to those who had been converted: Christians. He was saying that because we were now new creations and all things are new in Christ, we need to put those new things on and begin to walk, talk and act like Christ. We need to clothe ourselves in holiness. I was a new creation; my old sinful self died at the cross with Jesus and the new me (my new man) needed to come forth. The problem was that the old me (my old man) with his sin nature, or in my case, the old woman, wanted to come back from the dead and continue to rule as she had done in the past. Ephesians 2:3 says, "Among whom also we all had our conversation in times past in the lusts of our flesh, fulfilling the desires of the flesh and of the mind; and were by nature the children of wrath, even as others." I found that I not only had a problem with my old mindset, I also had a problem with my flesh or old woman.

This is why Paul pointed out in Ephesians 4:22 that we must first address our flesh. He said, "That ye put off concerning the former conversation the old man, which is corrupt according to the deceitful lusts..." The Greek word used in this scripture for "conversation" is "anastrophe" and it refers to non-verbal communication. The definition for this word, according to the Blue Letter Bible website reads: *manner of life, conduct, behavior and deportment.* Our English word "deportment" carries a meaning itself that has to do with a person's behavior or manners. Some of its synonyms are a person's practices, actions, and performances. In this case, the word "conversation" actually has little to do with verbal communication. Instead, it references non-verbal communication, actions, behavior and our lifestyles. Again, we can see that what a man thinks in his heart is closely connected to his actions. His old sinful self (his sin nature) adds to the struggle as well.

In Ephesians chapter four, the Apostle Paul offers a solution to this problem. Since our thoughts and "old man" dictate our actions and deeds, we are to "… be renewed in the spirit of our minds," that way, we can put on the new man. He instructs that we do this by dealing with our old self first, "That ye put off concerning the former conversation the old man, which is corrupt according to the deceitful lusts…"

This was the next factor which influenced my ungodly lifestyle as a born again believer. In my Christian walk, up until that season of my life, I had tried to live godlier, but because I didn't know the principles that I was now learning, I failed. Eventually, I just gave up and went back to living as I did before salvation. Over a period of time, I became desensitized to the Holy Spirit's conviction, thus, fooling myself into believing that I was living for Him, even though I had blatant sin in my life. The key for me was in understanding that this was another condition inherited from Adam, the first man.

Basically, my 'old man' (my sin nature) needed to be dealt with as well as my mind. When Adam sinned, not only did he lose his spiritual connection with God, he also lost the nature of God abiding in him. He then received sin in his very nature. Romans 5:19 confirms this thought, "For as by one man's disobedience many were made sinners..." Subsequently, all those after Adam inherited sin at the very fiber of their being.

David, the man who was after God's own heart, acknowledged this in Psalm 51, "Behold, I was shapen in iniquity; and in sin did my mother conceive me." David was saying that even before he was born, he was a sinner. His son, Solomon who, according to the Bible, was the wisest man who ever lived, agreed when he said in Ecclesiastes 7:20, "For there is not a just man upon earth, that doeth good, and sinneth not." All of Adam's offspring inherited this sin condition.

Paul states this fact in Romans 3:26, "For all have sinned, and come short of the glory of God." The glory of God is the expressed image of God. This is why we as believers must be conformed to the image of Christ. We were born without the image and nature of God, therefore, we were sinners before we had an opportunity to sin. This sin nature compels us to rebel against God, doing the opposite of what is right to do, especially when we make up our minds to do that which is right by God. In Romans 7:20, Paul said, "Now if I do what I do not want to do, it is no longer I who do it, but it is sin living in me that does it." In our pre-conversion state, there is very little we can do to control this behavior. But through this teaching, I discovered as Paul did that there is a solution in Christ!

Paul exclaims, in Romans 7:24-25 (AMP), "Wretched and miserable man that I am! Who will [rescue me and] set me free from this body of death [this corrupt, mortal existence]? Thanks be to God [for my deliverance] through Jesus Christ our Lord! So then, on the one hand I myself with my mind serve the law of God, but on the other, with my flesh [my human nature, my worldliness, my sinful capacity—I serve] the law of sin." Through Jesus, our old sin nature was dealt with at the cross and we were given a new nature through the Holy Spirit living in us. II Peter 1:4, confirms this fact when it stated, "Whereby are given unto us exceeding great and precious promises: that by these ye might be partakers of the divine nature..."

As far as I was concerned, there was a new sheriff in town: the person of the Holy Spirit; that divine nature! Romans 8:9 (TLB) declares, "You are controlled by your new nature if you have the Spirit of God living in you. (And remember that if anyone doesn't have the Spirit of Christ living in him, he is not a Christian at all…" I was most definitely a Christian and I was about to learn how to yield to the Spirit of God. As I would hand the care and rule of my life over to Him, I would be enabled to bring forth fruit that was pleasing to God. After all, I had made a commitment to follow Christ for the rest of my life this time.

The Bible teaches us how to bring our flesh under subjection to the Holy Spirit. Romans 8:12-14 reads, "Therefore, brethren, we are debtors, not to the flesh, to live after the flesh. For if ye live after the flesh, ye shall die: but if ye through the Spirit do mortify the deeds of the body, ye shall live. For as many as are led by the Spirit of God, they are the sons of God." The "sons of God" are Christians. As Christians, we are, in effect, living two lives on the earth. We have our natural life in the flesh and we are also living a spiritual life in the kingdom of God. When we get saved, we are to allow Christ to live through us in our natural lives. Otherwise, we would be living a life catering to our flesh. Allowing Christ to live through us is not an easy feat. We must begin to grow spiritually, learning how to follow the Spirit, rather than our flesh.

Up until this teaching, I was allowing the passions of my flesh to have its way in my life. For example, in my old life, I didn't have a problem with casual sex. Now that Jesus had become real to me, I was convicted of that lifestyle, but I had not been delivered from the spirit of lust at that time. Another example was the choice of language I would engage in, using a few "choice" words to express myself. Jesus's command to His disciples in Luke 9:23, was becoming even more plain to me. He said, "If any man will come after me, let him deny himself, and take up his cross daily, and follow me."

The practical side to this teaching of having my mind renewed was that, concerning this "old woman," I would daily have to mortify, crucify and choke her in order to keep her out of the way of what the Spirit was doing in my mindset. Paul said, "I die daily (see I Corinthians 15:31)." I had to make a decision to remind myself that the old Marilyn and her ways had passed away, and I needed to keep her in that condition so that Christ could live through me on a daily basis. I had to deny my flesh from whatever she wanted that was ungodly. Colossians 3:1 says, "Seek those things which are above, since you are risen with Christ. Mortify therefore your members which are upon the earth; fornication, uncleanness, inordinate affection, evil concupiscence and covetousness, which is idolatry."

Regarding sexual fornication, I was convicted of this behavior, but I continued to participate in it. I knew that it was wrong, however, I didn't believe that it was wrong. I found that my mind needed to be renewed in this area. The truth about my mindset was I believed that since other Christians engaged in premarital sex, that somehow, it was okay with God. Since my mind dictates what my body will do, I was allowing my flesh to dictate my actions. When I learned what the Bible teaches about fornication, I had to make a decision to believe it, come into repentance and begin to live as the Bible requires. To some degree, I had been waiting on God to deliver me. He was waiting for me to just stop fornicating. I found that when I did make the decision to stop, there was a grace helping me to indeed stop. This is how the Holy Spirit helps us to mortify the old man. Putting this knowledge into practice, I was eventually free from sexual sins. It wasn't easy, but as I persevered, relying on the self-control that the Holy Spirit provides us with, I overcame. Colossians 3:8 continues a list of what we should mortify. It reads, "To put off anger, wrath, malice, blasphemy, filthy communication out of your mouth." My mouth got saved as well.

In Galatians, we are given a list of deeds that helps us to know when we are not leaning on the Spirit, but living in our flesh. Galatians 5:19, "Now the works of the flesh are manifest, which are these; adultery, fornication, uncleanness, lasciviousness, Idolatry, witchcraft, hatred, variance, emulations, wrath, strife, seditions, heresies, envyings, murders, drunkenness, revellings, and such like…" When I took a good look at my life, I found that I had impure thoughts, a lust for worldly gain, jealousy and anger, plus, I was full of complaints and criticism. What really got my attention was when I found out that I had been participating in witchcraft, the occult and mysticism.

Yep, I didn't realize it until I came across a cross-referenced scripture in my study Bible. Deuteronomy 18:10-12 scared the socks off me. It reads, "There shall not be found among you any one that maketh his son or his daughter to pass through the fire, or that useth divination, or an observer of times, or an enchanter, or a witch. Or a charmer, or a consulter with familiar spirits, or a wizard, or a necromancer. For all that do these things are an abomination unto the Lord..." At that time in my life, I was consulting evil spirits because that's what reading horoscopes is. I was addicted to those little scrolls that they sell at the checkout counters of the grocery stores. I bought one on a daily basis. Like clockwork, I would read them and expect what they predicted about my life to come to pass. At last, the understanding came to me. I am to seek the Lord for instruction for my life and not witches. Also, in the ignorance of my youth on a few occasions, I had visited so-called palm readers, participated in séances and played with Ouija board games. I also had several mysticism and false religion books in my possession. Recognizing the sins of the flesh, I had to do some serious house cleaning. God was expecting me to take action; I knew that much. I immediately stopped buying and reading the horoscopes and I destroyed all of the demonic trinkets, books and clothing items I had in my possession. No matter what their value was, I destroyed them because they attracted demons. Next, I stood before God and repented for the sins of my youth, and finally, I denounced any alliances that I had inadvertently formed, including unholy soul ties with the demonic world because of my ignorance of having touched such unclean things. I didn't want to be an abomination to the Lord.

I was beginning to get my flesh together as I was allowing God to renew my mind. Romans 12:2-5 states the following, "And be not conformed to this world: but be ye transformed by the renewing of your mind, that ye may prove what is that good, and acceptable, and perfect, will of God." As I "put off the old man", what would help me to continue in this vein was to make a wholehearted commitment to exchanging those hindering thoughts and beliefs of mine for the mind of Christ. The Bible promises that there would be a reward for these very actions. Proverbs 16:2-3 (AMPC) reveals this truth, "All the ways of a man are pure in his own eyes, but the Lord weighs the spirits (the thoughts and intents of the heart). Roll your works upon the Lord [commit and trust them wholly to Him; He will cause your thoughts to become agreeable to His will, and] so shall your plans be established and succeed." Once again, the truth is that our actions in life directly correlate with our mindsets and thinking patterns. I was on my way to being transformed.

As I put off the works of the flesh, I began to put on the character of Christ in my inner man, the new self, through the renewing of my mind. In Colossians 3:1-9, we learn what to "put off." This statement relates to our sin nature and verses 10,12-14 tells us what we are to "put on." "And have put on the new man, which is renewed in knowledge after the image of him that created him: Put on therefore, as the elect of God, holy and beloved, bowels of mercies, kindness, humbleness of mind, meekness, longsuffering, forbearing one another and forgiving one another if any man have a quarrel against any: even as Christ forgave you, so also do ye. And above all these things put on charity, which is the bond of perfectness." These describe the character of Christ. Notice that in this scripture passage, the Bible teaches that the new man comes with knowledge of the image of Christ. We get that knowledge through the Holy Spirit and through the scriptures: the Word of God.

David said in Psalm 119:11, "Thy word have I hid in mine heart, that I might not sin against thee." There is something about hiding the Word in our hearts that gives us a readiness to withstand sin. James admonishes us to receive the Word. James 1:21, "Wherefore lay apart all filthiness and superfluity of naughtiness, and receive with meekness the engrafted word, which is able to save your souls." The Word, when engrafted into our hearts, is able to change our souls. Remember that our soul includes our mind, will and emotions. How is the Word 'engrafted' into our hearts? Another word we can use in place of "engrafted" is "implanted." Through the instruction from others, through preaching, through reading and through studying the Word, we are "'implanting" it into our hearts and mind. However, we must do a little more than just hear the Word; verse 22 says, "But be ye doers of the word, and not hearers only, deceiving your own selves." When we hear the Word, we must believe it, receive it and take action. Verse 23, further instructs us on this subject, "For if any be a hearer of the word, and not a doer, he is like unto a man beholding his natural face in a glass: For he beholdeth himself, and goeth his way, and straightway forgetteth what manner of man he was. But whoso looketh into the perfect law of liberty, and continueth therein, he being not a forgetful hearer, but a doer of the work, this man shall be blessed in his deed." The Word can serve as a mirror. The Word is Jesus, He became flesh and dwelt among us (see John 1:1-2,14). When we encounter the Word by hearing or reading it, we are able to see our own faults. We can see for ourselves where we don't line up with the character of Christ. The Word can correct our thinking, however, it's not until we begin to do what the Word instructs that our actions are changed. Wrong actions that have been changed into right actions are proof of repentance. Doing these things causes the Word to move from head knowledge to heart experience; this is what brings change to our minds and, subsequently, our actions and character. The power of the Word of God took on a whole new dimension in my life. I needed to be transformed.

Disciples of Christ are not to continue to "fashion" or "shape" ourselves according to our former ways of life because we have been predestined to be conformed to the image of Jesus Christ. We are to "put on the new man." We must live for God, yielding ourselves over to the Holy Spirit so that He can transform us into what God has called us to be. Thank God, we have the Spirit of God who enables us to do what we need to do in order to become successful. We are to fashion ourselves to His image with help from the Holy Spirit. II Corinthians 3:18 says, "But we all… are changed into the same image from glory to glory, even as by the Spirit of the Lord." He does this from the inside out, as evidenced in the following statement, "The inward man is renewed day by day" (see II Corinthians 4:16-17). Yes, there were a whole lot of thoughts that needed to be eradicated! There were belief systems and patterns of thinking that needed to be uprooted. Concerning my heart, those deeper thoughts needed to be uprooted as well. These were the things of my character that affected the inward man.

I was convinced that crucifying the old man and putting on the new man would require a transformation in my thought life. Satan had built a fortress around my mind; my thinking was enslaved to what I had been indoctrinated with. Not only did my thoughts directly affect sin in my life, but they also affected how I saw myself. I had beliefs about myself that were imposed upon me by others and their views of my life and future. These perceptions were based on circumstances that could only be seen with the natural eyes. For example, while growing up, I remember overhearing a conversation held between some adult family members and they were discussing my siblings and I and the fact that we were orphans. One of them said something to the effect of, "Well, those kids don't have much of a chance in life under these circumstances." I'm sure that I heard the comment out of the context in which it had been spoken; however, this affected my young mind. During this season of soul searching, I identified a pattern in my life directly connected to this belief. I was one who often sabotaged opportunities to advance in life by disqualifying myself. This action was rooted in what I had heard and believed. I had internalized the belief that I didn't have much of a chance in life. As Marilyn thought in her heart, so was she. I became a person who could not recognize opportunity. I recognized the need for change.

I needed to do two things: bring my flesh into subjection to God and have my mind renewed so that I could put on the mind of Christ. I would begin a lifetime journey with the Holy Spirit since He would be the one to rely upon. I was glad for this teaching, otherwise, I would have long since drifted away from the things of God yet again. I was up for the challenge.

Chapter Nine

<u>Deep Healing: Heart Matters: Transformation</u>

"But let it be the hidden man of the heart, in that which is not corruptible, even the ornament of a meek and quiet spirit, which is in the sight of God of great price."
1 Peter 3:4

One of the things that became of value to me was my inward appearance because this is what is of great value to God. I had a desire to please God. After having experienced the teaching from Ephesians 4:22-24, I realized that beauty comes from within. It comes from an inner thought life that has been renewed and a heart that has been purified. Peter 3:3-4 says, "Whose adorning let it not be that outward adorning of plaiting the hair, and of wearing of gold, or of putting on of apparel; but let it be the hidden man of the heart, in that which is not corruptible, even the ornament of a meek and quiet spirit, which is in the sight of God is of great price."

I had come to terms that in some regard, I had been living a very hypocritical life. I was a surface Christian, caring more about what people thought of my outward appearance than whether or not God was pleased with my inward appearance. In Psalm 51:6, King David said, "Behold, You desire truth in the inward parts. And in the hidden part You will make me to know wisdom." I had become willing to face the truth about any part of myself that needed to be changed. I declared to God as David did in verse 10 of the same passage, "Create in me a clean heart, O God, and renew a steadfast spirit within me."

I knew that it would take God's wisdom to renew my heart. Jeremiah 17:9-10 declares this about our mind and heart, "The heart is deceitful above all things, and desperately wicked: who can know it?" I was coming to terms with the fact that there were some dark emotional issues lodged in the deepest parts of my heart and I would not be able to figure them out on my own. Verse 10 points to the solution, "I the Lord search the heart, I try the reins, even to give every man according to his ways, and according to the fruit of his doings."

I needed the Holy Spirit to get to the heart of things because only He could show me the hidden matters of my heart. After all, He is the Spirit of God's truth and He was about to help me face truth. I had become willing to face the good, the bad and the ugly about myself. I made a decision that I was going to stop letting the past haunt me, so I put myself, my heart and my thoughts in the hands of the living God for correction.

It is a helpless, painful and lonely place to be in the hand of God's correction. He has to open your eyes to your ugly and that hurts. At the very least, it's uncomfortable. His love at work through correction (see Hebrews 12:6). I didn't always want to see what He was showing me about myself, so I would deny it for a season. Pride, selfishness and rebellion all boil down to spiritual immaturity. They are oftentimes the reasons we don't always yield over to God when He corrects us. I've come to understand that you only prolong the trial when you are unwilling to go through the process.

I had to allow God to dig deep and go deep. During this long process, sometimes, it would be only a superficial cutting away because that's all I could take at the time. At other times, it would be a pruning. Sometimes a purging took place. Lastly, an uprooting would take place; an uprooting is the event that precedes permanent transformation. I found that one of the keys to having the mind renewed was in hiding the Word of God in my heart. When Joshua was to lead the new generation of Israel into the promised land, God gave him the following instructions in Joshua 1:8, "This book of the law shall not depart out of thy mouth; but thou shalt meditate therein day and night, that thou mayest observe to do according to all that is written therein: for then thou shalt make thy way prosperous, and then thou shalt have good success." Because of this instruction from God, I began to spend more time meditating on the scriptures that pertained to what the Holy Spirit was doing in me at the time. I began to speak those things that I needed to put into practice. Second Corinthians 10:4-5 reads, "(For the weapons of our warfare are not carnal, but mighty through God to the pulling down of strong holds;) Casting down imaginations, and every high thing that exalteth itself against the knowledge of God, and bringing into captivity every thought to the obedience of Christ."

Since I needed to practice bringing my thoughts into subjection to Christ, I meditated on the aforementioned scriptures and was reminded that the Devil had succeeded in building strongholds in my mind. In this particular season in my life, those strongholds would have to be destroyed; they'd have to be annihilated!

What I knew was that I needed to undergo a deep cleaning, deep uprooting and deep deliverance to embrace a change that was not superficial. I needed a permanent change. I began to pick up my sword of the Spirit: the Word of God (see Ephesians 6:17), and I began to pull down the strongholds in my mind daily. I went on prayer walks and confessed the Word of God over myself. I went in my prayer closet and decreed the Word. When I was driving, I listened to the Word.

Another tool God used during this season was my habit of journaling my thoughts on a regular basis. I believe that journaling, or writing in a diary (as some call it) helped to save me from literally losing my mind as a young adult. However, this teaching revolutionized my journaling discipline.

When I got out on my own, I realized that I was bombarded with a lot of unhealthy thoughts, memories, and feelings from my past. I was one who kept things bottled up inside. I didn't share my deep concerns, thoughts or what I was feeling with others. On one hand, I was an extreme introvert, and on the opposite hand, I was an extrovert. When something traumatic happened in my life, I didn't share it with anyone. I just kept to my finely tuned routine. I had created a mental file I like to call "Marilyn's Troubles and Woes." The subtitle could have been: "Everything that Has Come in My Life to Harm, Abuse, And Disappoint Me..." I kept this file neatly tucked away in the deepest pockets of my heart, but not so deep that I couldn't easily access it; I kept it deep enough to where no one could detect that it was there. Once neatly tucked away in the most secret area of my heart, I would then throw a rug over it. This rug served as a covering so that if anyone were to get a peek into my heart, they wouldn't be able to see my file.

I guess one could call that rug a veil or a mask. I called it my happy because I needed to be reminded to be happy in spite of my circumstances. This "happy" was my extroverted self; it was the mask I wore to get through my young and inexperienced life. After a while, in order to enhance the effectiveness of my mask, I decorated it with drugs, cigarettes, alcohol, and promiscuous behavior.

I began journaling my thoughts because it was a matter of survival. I had become so full of grief that I ran out of room to store it all in my heart, so I took to journaling. The knowledge I received from the teaching about renewing the mind woke me up. Since I was paying attention to my thoughts on purpose, I began to notice just how dark they were whenever I began to journal. Quite frankly, they were depressing. The

Holy Spirit was beginning to move me into the place of healing and deliverance. I was coming to realize just how deep into my thought life I needed to go. I realized that it was time to lift up that rug and really look at what was under it. It was time to take an inventory of my heart and to become truly accountable for what was there.

God needed me to trust that He knew how to heal me. Additionally, He needed me to know what it would take to adjust my perceptions of life to His perceptions. Up until this point, my perceptions were based on my own imperfectly formed thoughts, from opinions of others to the Devil's lies. I was getting ready to go into deep waters by revisiting painful childhood memories. Unbeknown to me, these memories were causing me to falter in my faith walk because I kept tripping over the roots they created. God reminded me that I had been delivered from the indwelling demons of shame, unworthiness, and rejection, plus, on two other occasions, I had been delivered from the spirits of lust, condemnation, and anger. My thoughts correlated with these demonic personalities. What I mean by this is that I could see where spiritual doors were open in my life, allowing those demons to gain access to me.

For example, one such memory was when I was in middle school. There was a certain teacher who volunteered to mentor me and a group of my friends. One day, when we were all gathered together, she asked me a very personal and embarrassing question in front of my peers. She said to me, "Marilyn, where is your mother?" This was painful. I felt like someone had taken a knife and stabbed me in the heart. I didn't know how to respond because I didn't know where my mother was. At the time, I had the impression that she had known more about my mother than I had. All I knew was that one day my mother dropped us off at a babysitter's house and I hadn't seen her again for a few years. One day, after I returned home from school, she came through the door. When I saw her, I cried out to her saying, "Mommy", but as my eyes fixed on her, I could tell something was different about her. I would later come to understand the hard reality that my mother had suffered a nervous breakdown. Consequently, she had been diagnosed with schizophrenia and manic depression. As quickly as she had come back into our lives, she departed our lives yet again.

I didn't know where my mother was, plus, how does someone who is not used to sharing her feelings give an answer to a question like that? I don't know why my teacher asked that question, but I do know that it wasn't to build my self-esteem because she never approached me with that subject again. So, in my mind, I was left with the stigma of being motherless and fatherless. I knew where my father was. He had become hooked on heroine and was serving time in prison. It probably didn't matter one way or the other with my friends. It was no secret that four of my six siblings and I lived with my grandmother. However, for me, that question brought back the painful memory of that dreadful day when, at the first sight of my mother, I knew something was wrong with her, even before she said a word.

That question also solidified the reality that my mother wasn't around and I didn't know where she was. This is when the Devil really began to play with my mind. I began to take on self-perceptions like, "I'm less than because I don't have a mother." The question left me vulnerable to my own vain imaginations. No one knew that I was battling thoughts of depression. My exterior was thriving. I was a cheerleader, gifted in athletics, a good student and my friends were some of the most popular kids in school. Inwardly, I wanted to hide because the less attention I received, the safer I felt.

I was ashamed of my life. I was embarrassed because of my mother's illness and because my father wasn't around. Needless to say, shame had come into my heart much earlier in my life. Throughout my childhood, I had been molested by various people, and when I was eight or nine years old, I had been raped by two young men. There is a certain amount of grief and shock that comes to a child who's been sexually abused, regardless of what type of abuse they've endured, but there is also an enormous amount of shame to deal with. Again, I was the type that held everything in. I wasn't willing to talk to anyone about what had happened to me, so there could be no counseling.

Consequently, I didn't receive the wisdom on what to do with my feelings, so I mastered the art of tucking grief away. I got so good at it that I convinced myself that I was okay. I was resilient, it would seem.

However, shame followed me into high school and into college. In college, I found out that I was pregnant. After having undergone an abortion, another level of shame came upon me along with a bunch of unstable emotions. This shame was the culprit behind me drinking and eventually picking up the habit of smoking on my college campus. I was so ashamed of myself that I became socially shy. I found that whenever I had a drink, my inhibitions went away and I could then be myself, whoever that was. Shame caused me to want to live in secret. I really didn't want to be close to anyone, because I feared they would find out the secrets of my life, and I had a lot of them. I didn't want anyone to get a glimpse at what was in my heart. Of course, at the time, I didn't understand that to be the case.

I felt abandoned by my parents. Abandonment brings rejection and rejection set in for me. When rejection sets in, the door for self-rejection follows and truthfully, this is a form of self-hatred. When people are rejected, they are oftentimes convinced that something is wrong with them. They think to themselves, "If this person rejected me, there must be something wrong with me." This opens the door for self-rejection and self-hatred. This was my experience. To some degree, I rejected myself and this attracted a spirit of unworthiness. Rejection, unworthiness and shame, along with other equally persuasive variables helped to convince me to have an abortion. After all, how could I have anything worth anything? The Devil really had a grip on my young mind.

Anger took hold of me as well. After my teacher asked me that humiliating question, I was sent to the principal's office the very next day for acting out in class. Up until that point, I didn't even know what the inside of our school's office looked like since I had never gotten into trouble at school. I knew that I was angry; I felt different. I wasn't angry at my mother, father or anyone else. I was angry because I just didn't understand my situation and no one took the time to explain anything to me. So, I just tucked all my feelings into that deep place in my heart. This left me vulnerable to my own thoughts and my own perceptions concerning everything. I set out to find the truth on my own. I didn't do this intentionally; that's just what we humans do, whether we realize it or not. My inexperienced and youthful reasoning looked at the facts, and the fact was I didn't have parents but all my friends did. I was convinced that this put me at a disadvantage. My perception was that I was disadvantaged, so I began to put myself on the demerit system.

"You don't have a father; take one point away."
"You don't have a mother; take another point away.

"You have a mother, but she's ill; take two points away."
"You don't have a family car; take another point away."
"You don't have new clothes; take another point away."

These types of calculations went on and on throughout high school and even into college.

This is how the Holy Spirit helped me. Philippians 4:6-7 gives us this promise of peace. "Be careful for nothing; but in every thing by prayer and supplication with thanksgiving let your requests be made known unto God. And the peace of God, which passeth all understanding, shall keep your hearts and minds through Christ Jesus." This is a scripture that I had meditated on throughout the duration of this teaching series. By this time, I had memorized it; it was "engrafted" into my heart. One day, while reading a recent entry in my journal, I was prompted by the Holy Spirit. I asked myself this question, "Do you have this kind of peace that keeps your heart and mind beyond your understanding?" I agreed that I did have this kind of peace. The next question that I asked myself got my attention, "Why are you still anxious then?" At that moment, I was confronted with a truth I couldn't deny. What I was reading in my journal at the time proved that I was indeed anxious, unhappy and wanting. I realized in this moment that there was a difference between what's on your mind and what's in your heart. In all those years of writing, my journal had basically served as a record of what was on my mind at the time; it was just a stream of consciousness. Thinking about this brought me to the conclusion that my thoughts were the manifestations or the fruit of the deeper matters of my heart. I had rarely dealt with the root causes which were the deeper things of my heart, that place where my files were hidden. As I perused through some of my earlier journals, I found that there were occasions when I addressed some of the issues written in my files but never any occasion where I had arrived at a productive solution. Basically, I had done a lot of "surface" writing.

I knew that the kind of peace this passage of scripture described was a peace that settles all inner disturbances. The Greek word for peace is "eirēnē," from which we get the English name "Irene." One of the *Blue Letter Bible* website definitions is: "of Christianity, the tranquil state of a soul assured of its salvation through Christ, and so fearing nothing from God and content with its earthly lot, of whatsoever sort that is." I was sure that I had most of this peace that the aforementioned definition describes. I felt assured of my salvation and I feared nothing from God. However, I had to ask myself if I sincerely had that soul contentment with my "lot in life." I couldn't honestly answer yes to this question. I concluded that I could not claim that I had the fullness of God's peace working in my life. I knew that it was available to me, but I honestly couldn't claim that I was fully benefiting from it because my thoughts were full of conflict and unrest concerning my "lot in life": my past.

The phrase, "let your request be made known unto God" came to mind and turned out to be the key to me experiencing the full gamut of the peace Jesus offers us in this earthly life. The fullest meaning of this phrase actually has to do with not just asking for things from God in prayer, but entering into an intimate communication with Him. During prayer, we are to talk to God about what is going on in our lives, bringing everything before Him and having an open discussion with Him about them. It's not that we are telling Him anything new. God knows all things about us, including what is in our hearts and what is on our minds. When Jesus taught His disciples to pray, He told them that the Father knoweth what things they needed even before they asked (see Matthew 6:8). In fact, God knows a lot about us according to Psalm 139: 1-3. It reads, "O LORD, You have searched me and known me. You know my sitting down and my rising up; You understand my thought afar off. For there is not a word on my tongue, But behold, O LORD, You know it altogether." What David acknowledged in this Psalm was that the LORD saw his every move, knew what was on his mind and knew the words on his tongue, even before David made a move, thought a thought or spoke a word.

I was getting it. God knew me, but I didn't know me. I needed to know myself, the real me. I couldn't know me unless the real me got free. I realized that as long as I held on to that file, I would not be free and that my power would be in the hands of those who robbed me in the past. I had to search out my own heart as the Lord had already done so.

One day, I was sharing these thoughts with my friend Cyndi. After listening intently as she always did, she simply said to me, "You must lay yourself bare before God." She quoted Hebrews 4:13. The NIV version of this scripture reads, "Nothing in all creation is hidden from God's sight. Everything is uncovered and laid bare before the eyes of him to whom we must give account." She gave me the example of a lobster ready to be eaten. After it is cracked open, the meat that is inside is laid bare. She went on to say that even though God sees all things, we need to come and lay ourselves bare before Him willingly becoming transparent vessels.

From my friend's analogy, I understood that I needed to first be "cracked open" before I could "lay myself bare" before the Lord. I was hiding and until I took off the mask and began to go deeper with God, I would never be free. I was confronted with a choice. It goes back to the wealth of understanding I was getting from the teaching series. I have a body (my flesh) that houses my spirit and soul. My spirit is where God, the Holy Spirit abides in me. My soul encompasses my mind, my emotions and my will. I was living a fleshly Christian life because I was allowing my emotions and intellect to determine my will or choices in life. I was responding to the circumstances in my life from my flesh. Judging from my journal entrances, I was a very emotional person. I clearly saw that my decisions in life were based on my own preconceived notions and emotions, and if I didn't confront my past, I would continue to be imprisoned to my soul (mind and emotions). My heart had become hardened and callused from bitterness. God, though He knew what was in my heart, couldn't change me unless I was willing to open up to Him. The good news is that I had a choice and I chose to allow the Holy Spirit to show me the way to freedom. First, I needed to be cracked open. I needed to find the anointing to do so.

I needed to go to the oil press as Jesus did. The Garden of Gethsemane was filled with beautifully kept olive trees; it's Aramaic name was the garden of the oil press. In Jesus's day, an oil press was used to crush the olives to get the oil from them. The oil from the olive represents the anointing. Jesus overcame His emotions because the tremendous pressure He underwent in the garden brought forth the anointing. The anointing assisted Him in giving His will over to the Father during His prayers in the Garden of Gethsemane. Luke 22:44 details His struggle, "And being in an agony he prayed more earnestly: and his sweat was as it were great drops of blood falling down to the ground." According to the Strong's Concordance, the definition for the

Greek word *"agōnia,"* from which we get our English word "agony," implies severe mental struggles and emotions; they reference agony and anguish. In Matthew 26:38, Jesus describes His struggle in the garden in the following manner, "My soul is exceeding sorrowful, even unto death..." The phrase, *"perilypos" literally means 'exceedingly sorrowful,"* and this definition means that He was intensely sad and overcome with a sorrow so intense that it could cause one's death. This would explain how His sweat looked like great drops of blood.

I don't know about anyone else, but I have definitely experienced severe emotional struggles and agony causing me to feel like I wanted to die. In fact, I wanted to die at one point, so I attempted to take my own life. Of course, I overcame because of God's grace and through no effort of my own. However, God didn't want me to go back to that place of emotional dilemma ever again, and quite frankly, neither did I.

Jesus overcame His struggle through praying the same prayer three times on that night saying, "O my Father, if it be possible, let this cup pass from me: nevertheless, not as I will, but as thou wilt" (Matthew 26:39). Each time, He prayed more intensely than before. In the garden is where Jesus overcame the temptation of His flesh and own emotions, and it was necessary for Him to do so. If He hadn't, He would not have been able to stay on that cross. When He found them sleeping in the garden, rather than praying, He gave the following instructions to His disciples. Matthew 26:41 reads, "Watch and pray, that ye enter not into temptation: the spirit indeed is willing, but the flesh is weak." We know that Jesus is God, both fully divine and fully man. If he was fully man, this would mean that Jesus faced temptations just as we do in life. Hebrews 2:8 confirms this; it reads, "For in that he himself hath suffered being tempted, he is able to succour them that are tempted." We find Jesus on His knees, humbled before the Father during His hour of temptation. Jesus overcame the temptation to back out of His commitment to fulfill God's will for His life before going to the cross. Matthew 26:45, "Then cometh he to his disciples, and saith unto them, Sleep on now, and take your rest: behold, the hour is at hand, and the Son of man is betrayed into the hands of sinners." While Judas was betraying Him, Jesus was undergoing tremendous grief and sorrow. But this tremendous pressure squeezed the anointing oil out of Him. He gained peace concerning His lot in life, which was the cross, and He handed His will over to the Father through earnest prayer.

It was settled then. I needed to go to the garden of the oil press for the anointing. The tremendous amount of struggle with my past would actually bring forth the anointing needed to conquer my own will. I would then be able to pick up my cross and follow Jesus for the rest of my life, doing it God's way just as Jesus did.

Journaling had become my garden of Gethsemane. It was the crushing tool that God used to press the oil of anointing out of me. I needed the anointing to face my lot in life; I had to effectively pick up my cross to follow Jesus. The Holy Spirit coached me into approaching and addressing the condition of my heart on a regular basis. I had to confront the truth and stop running from it. I would have to face my emotional sorrows and dilemmas as I pulled out my journal daily or stepped into my prayer closet.

God prepared some things way in advance of this season in my life. He had already dealt with my proverbial rug, or better yet, the covering I used to disguise my heart with. He had long since exposed it when He delivered me from drugs, alcohol and promiscuity. I had been free of these habits, but not from the mindset that accompanied that bondage. All I needed to do was to do away with that rug and begin to lay my innermost being bare before the Lord.

My journaling became more productive, helping me to find resolve and healing. Over a period of time, as I would go to my Gethsemane, the Holy Spirit would meet me there and give me instructions. First, I would have to face the facts; I would have to accept the truth. It was sort of like filing a case against someone without having to face them. Instead, I would face God and tell Him the whole truth as I knew it to be.

For example, the truth was that I had been molested. It was real, it did happen and no one could take it back. I had to accept that as my reality. Secondly, I would have to name the guilty parties. I made a list of all of those involved, even those whose negligence played a part in me being molested. Whether I was right or wrong in my accusation, it was imperative to list everyone I held to blame. I was telling God my version of the story.

Next, I needed to determine the extent of the injury done to me. This was done through answering a series of questions God had presented me with. I carefully thought about each answer, answering them with as much detail as I possibly could. How did this act against me harm me? What did I lose because of it? How did it change me? Once again, the answers were my truth. The point was that I was challenged to search out my heart from my perspective. It was about laying myself bare before God.

These questions opened the door for personal discovery. I found that I had anger, hatred and unforgiveness in my heart towards my attackers and everyone else who I held to blame. I was surprised to discover a root of bitterness toward the mother of my attackers and my own mother as well. I was angry with their mother because I blamed her for raising them to be the monsters that they were. I blamed my mother for allowing such a family into our lives and for using them as our babysitters. Nevertheless, I realized that my mother was very young and inexperienced in life at that time, and she had her own set of problems.

The Lord began to minister to me concerning my mother and I found His words to be comforting. He said that it was very important to hold my mother responsible for her negligence for two reasons: compromise and unforgiveness. If I was willing to give my mother a "pass" for her part, I would be compromising the truth. Calling her innocent, when in fact, she was guilty from my perspective, meant there could be no closure and no forgiveness. I definitely had unforgiveness in my heart towards my mother concerning this thing. I loved my mother and the thought of her mental condition brought deep emotional anguish; this added to my conflicted thoughts. But these were all reasons that I needed to bravely stand and tell God that she was guilty. Not doing so meant that there was no reason to forgive her. There was definitely anger in my heart towards her; I had a need to forgive.

This wisdom from God helped me with other cases and issues that were in my file. My father, for example. I had the same mixed emotions concerning him regarding areas in my life where I felt that he had failed. I had to separate the facts from my emotions in order to permanently forgive him. Oftentimes, when we say that we have forgiven someone, the enemy will come and play on our emotions, tricking us into believing we have forgiven someone that we have not forgiven. This causes us to go on an emotional roller coaster with that person. Sometimes, we like them and at other times, we don't. Emotional healing can only come after forgiveness.

God walked me through forgiveness for each person, especially for my father and mother. He showed me that when I hold a person guilty of something that they have done to me, it's like saying to God that they owe me something. In fact, I was holding them in debt to me. He had me take a look at the list of personal injuries I'd sustained and determine what harm and what loss I felt had incurred from each case. How was I changed? Then, He reasoned with me. Can any of your abusers give back to you what you have lost? Reality set in; I had been raped and my virginity had been taken. The rapist couldn't give me my innocence back. My father and mother couldn't turn back the hands of time and do the things they had failed to do a second time around. That old boyfriend who put extreme pressure on me to have sex with him and then broke up with me could not fix the pieces of my heart that he had broken. All the apologies in the world could not give back to me what was taken. Because the assaults themselves, whether emotional, physical or psychological became spiritual issues once they were done. Only God can heal a broken heart. Only God knows my intimate thoughts enough to be able to tell me how to become sound in my thinking and be emotionally stable yet again.

He said "Daughter, either you can continue to look to these people on your list to make you whole again or you can choose to let them go free, release them from their debt to you and look to me to recompense what you have lost. Please take into consideration that if you demand recompense from people, you will prevent your own healing and deliverance." As I made a heartfelt, conscious and educated decision to forgive, God led me in a beautiful repentance and forgiveness prayer based on Matthew 18:23-35, which detailed the parable of the unforgiving servant. I acknowledged the unforgiveness in my heart to God and then confessed to Him that I chose to release everyone on my list; I would release them from my heart, free of debt and owing me nothing. In so doing, each case I had against anyone was handed over to God to do with whatever He saw fit. God closed each case and handed me the victory.

Forgiveness of others is a prescription for a hardened heart. For my willingness to forgive, I received the compassion for people that Jesus had. I've heard the popular cliches, "hurt people hurt people" and "people can only do what they know to do." God even pointed out to me that my parents had their own issues in life and the way things turned out for us as children was in no way a reflection of their love or lack thereof for their children. Having gone through this process has birthed a gift of mercy in me that helps me to love people and bear with them beyond their faults.

God's way is effective. He took me through this process with each person that I once considered guilty, regardless of whether it was an uncle, aunt, cousin, sibling, friend, acquaintance, neighbor, old boyfriend, cat or dog. For whatever reason, whether big or small, I needed to come, lay myself bare before God and let Him settle each case once and for all in my mind. It was about coming to God and telling Him everything about everything. I was emptying myself of my old thought life by letting myself get intimate with God.

On the subject of molestation and rape, I realized that no one was ever held accountable for their actions against me; in the back of my mind, this had bothered me over the years. As I searched out my feelings about this, I noticed that these thoughts directly affected my self-esteem. I had not gotten justice; my feeling was that no one had counted me worthy of justice. I could see how this thought fed into rejection. I had identified a stronghold and God's response destroyed it. He reminded me of Romans 12:19, "Dearly beloved, avenge not yourselves, but rather give place unto wrath: for it is written, 'Vengeance is mine; I will repay, saith the Lord.'"

God would then replace those negative thoughts with His thoughts flowing from my heart into my mind. This was a benefit of having hidden the Word in my heart. I felt God saying, "I see man's motive and intent of the heart. I will give him according to his deeds. Since I'm not willing that any should perish, my wrath is designed to bring an evil heart into repentance. You must not live as the world does: an eye for an eye and a tooth for a tooth, but you shall pray for your enemies and those who have offended you. Do good to them who harm you, for it is like pouring a heap of coal upon their heads. Overcome evil by doing good. You must forgive because I have forgiven you." As I put these truths into action, I literally felt the grip Satan had on my heart released.

The more I searched out my deepest thoughts, the more I identified strongholds. God's Word was always right there to destroy the lie in my mind and replace it with His truth. For example, the Devil had used an ex-boyfriend of mine to build a stronghold in my mind, and this stronghold attacked my self-confidence and self-reliance. It was during a very hard time in my life when I had been using drugs, I was jobless and I had no means of taking care of myself. I relied completely on him. One day, my ex said, "You will never be able to take care of yourself; you will always need me." I hadn't realized how much I had internalized what this man had said. I actually bought into this lie. However, God reminded me of these words because He was ready to utterly destroy the stronghold the enemy had over my mind.

As I looked back at my past patterns, I discovered that I had been living under the dictates of dependency for some time, even before my ex had ever spoken those words to me. The Devil had merely used him to reinforce his stronghold. I discovered that I had actually grown up in a lifestyle of having to depend on people.

Because of the crisis that my siblings and I were cast into as orphans, we had no other choice but to accept help from others. Whether it was from the government, family members, well-meaning neighbors and even school teachers. Growing up in my grandmother's house with no family car, I watched her rely on an uncle or an aunt to come and take her to the grocery store or to run errands week after week. We would have to ask the parents of friends and neighbors for rides home in order to participate in after school programs. We received second hand clothes from family members and neighbors. At Christmas time, some of our more generous family members would pitch in to buy us presents. We would receive "secret Santa" gifts and toys from local programs for underprivileged families.

I'm definitely not complaining about these things. Thank God for people willing to help those in need and for programs set up to help families in crisis. These helped to make our lives a little better in the time of need. This was the point God was making. The problem that I was faced with was that to some degree I still had a stronghold of dependency when I was quite capable of living independent of people.

Because of this mindset, I attracted people in my life based on what they could do for me or how I could depend on them. I looked back at some of the men, friends and associates I had in my life at one time or another. I couldn't deny the truth. I was compelled to admit to God that I needed to be free from the "welfare" mentality.

I learned through this experience that with God, there is no shame in admitting the truth. We all fall short of God's standard in some way or another, whether we want to admit it to ourselves or not. The shame is in coming to the reality of the truth and not being willing to do anything about it. Subsequently, there would be many things about myself that I would have to take responsibility for as well. I would have to face the truth about choices I had made in life and accept the consequences for those choices.

There is something about repentance and confession that frees a soul from bondage. I John 1:9-10 gives us this promise, "If we confess our sins, he is faithful and just to forgive us our sins, and to cleanse us from all unrighteousness. If we say that we have not sinned, we make him a liar, and his word is not in us." As I stood yet again in the presence of God, this time admitting the manner of woman that I was and owning up to the truth about my character flaws, God responded to me with His Word. This was His way of letting me know that I was forgiven and set free. He began to purge my heart of unrighteous beliefs.

His Word came in a stream from His heart to mine, and then out of my mouth. This form of declaration was becoming a habit. I would often declare the following scriptures:

"And God is able to make all grace abound toward you; that ye, always having all sufficiency in all things, may abound to every good work" (II Corinthians 9:8).

"But my God shall supply all your need according to his riches in glory by Christ Jesus" (Philippians 4:19).

"Not that we are sufficient of ourselves to think any thing as of ourselves; but our sufficiency is of God" (II Corinthians 3:5).

"I can do all things through Christ which strengtheneth me" (Philippians 4:13).

I found that I had confessed what God says about me. He had cleansed me from the unrighteous thoughts that the devil had planted in me and replaced them with the very words I had been meditating on. I was experiencing the power of the Word of God engrafted in my heart. I had the key to a renewed mind.

I was finally finding a voice for myself and I was beginning to feel free. My thoughts were becoming more focused and productive. The next series of questions challenged me to confront the truth about my responsibilities. I would have to ask myself how I responded to what was done to me. My answer to this question (in particular), revealed to me the mentality of victimization. From my perspective, there wasn't much I could do as a child, therefore, I was a victim. Anyone with a victim mentality is enslaved to that false reality. I also realized that I held a certain amount of blame on myself, as most who suffer from sexual abuse does. As I confronted these truths, I called them what they were: tragedies. I practiced two steps: I accepted what I couldn't change and made a commitment to leave them in my past. I had to also daily confess over myself, John 8:36, "Whom the Son sets free is free indeed" and Romans 8:37, "I am more than a conqueror through Him that loved us."

I had to respond to the next series of questions God presented to me. How does abuse still affect me? What is unhealthy or counterproductive about the way it affected me? Giving careful thought to my answers, I wrote my conclusion in my journal. The act of the abuse and those who abused me still had power over me. I had allowed them to control my life. In my heart of hearts, I had somehow accepted that because my abusers trampled on my sexuality, I was not of value, and of course, that was a lie. To some degree, promiscuity is a product of having been molested and raped. Promiscuity is also a cause for unwanted pregnancies. Unwanted pregnancies are not a justification for abortion. Jesus said, "You will know the truth and the truth makes you free" (see John 8:32).

There is something about the truth, especially if it's an ugly one, that motivates you to want to become free. I was determined to be an overcomer, so I chose to do what it took to recover my life. I knew that I had been forgiven of all my sins since I had become a Christian, however, repentance was necessary. The hard reality was that I needed to own up to the truth: I did not value myself. It was certainly unfair that I had been molested, raped and treated inappropriately as a child. Now that I was a grown woman, I could no longer use those acts to justify my sin. As long as I stayed under the mentality of victimization, I would remain blinded from my moral obligations. I had to come before God as I had done with every truth I had been confronted with. I had to confess that I was a murderer; I had participated in abortions. I agreed with the Holy Spirit as He showed me how selfish I had been and that I had in turn become like my attackers. This was hard to accept, but it was the truth. I had to look at the facts and not at my emotions. Abortion was a selfish act born from low self-esteem and rejection of self. After repentance, I was delivered from the spirit of death and the stronghold associated with abortions.

Abuse brings much grief and sorrow to a person, but it also changes them. It's one of the things the Devil uses to superimpose his will for our lives over the will of the Father. When we put closure to what tragedies and grievances came on us in our lives and take responsibility for our parts, we close the door on the enemy. We allow God to put us in the position to gain back our authority and dominion over our lives.

Little by little, I began to take control over my thought life and bring it under the subjection of the Holy Spirit. This was the manner of my recovery: confronting the truth, acknowledging the facts, accepting what I could not change and doing something about what I could change. Recovery was summed up in these two words: resolve and closure.

During this period of time, a great healing had come to me. God showed me soul ties that needed to be broken. Ungodly mindsets, issues of fear, discouragement and passive aggressive behavior had fallen off me. God began to show me who He desired me to be. I began to speak over myself those things God had said about me. Deliverance also came through much fasting and praying. It didn't happen all at once, but it happened over a period of time.

As I went through a season of fasting, the Holy Spirit led me to write powerful prayers of deliverance, daily confessions and declarations for myself. He was teaching me how to warfare for myself, and at the same time, preparing me for my destiny. He reminded me of a conversation I had with Him when I was a child. Standing at the end of my grandmother's dirt-filled driveway and waiting for the school bus, I had entered into a conversation with myself. When God reminded me of this conversation, I realized that it wasn't a conversation with self, but with the unseen God. I was disgruntled about something, but I cannot remember what. I said, "When I grow up, I'm going to help disadvantaged girls like myself." Truthfully, at the age that I was, I don't know where the word "disadvantaged" came from. I'm certain that God impressed upon me to say this. I was confessing my future. There was another occasion where I had a conversation with a soothing voice coming from without. I had to be about four or five years old and I had fallen into a trance. I can not remember what the voice said to me, but after that experience, I can recall the joy I had. I was running around and repeating, "I can't wait until I grow up." I'm sure whatever was said to me, had to do with my destiny and I had said "yes" to that voice.

These were healing moments for me because I realized that God had been with me. Through everything that I had been through, He had been keeping me. Some of the things that I went through should have left me dead or in prison. Those things were just not my lots in life and I'm grateful to God for His grace. Nevertheless, what I survived is a testimony that God is real. Before He placed me in my mother's womb, God saw a need in the world, and He created me to fulfill that need. I'm not a mistake, even though some people mistreated me when I was vulnerable.

God has turned what the enemy tried to use to destroy me for my good and for the good of others. Those two conversations I had with God when I was a child proved that God was for me all along. Where I stand in life today is evidence. I'm able to share my testimony of how I have overcome my past with others to help them overcome their pasts.

God wants us to be better and stronger, especially those of us who have been victimized. I no longer allow my former circumstances to define who I am in a negative way. I've taken my freedom back and I am free to be who I was born to be. This defines the next step in our salvation. After becoming a new creation, we must set out to get our minds recovered from our pasts so that we can be free to pursue our callings in life.

The apostle Paul said in Philippians 3:13-14, "Brethren, I count myself to have apprehended: but this one thing I do, forgetting those things which are behind, and reaching forth unto those things which are before, I press toward the mark for the prize of the high calling of God in Christ Jesus." Like Paul, nowadays, I let the past be the past and it no longer can affect me in a negative way. I left my past on the other side of my salvation. I let today be today, and I find that because I'm healed from my past, I can bear the burdens of today without becoming overwhelmed. I let the future be the future because I trust that the Lord has a good plan for my life. I haven't mastered, nor have I become perfect in my doings, but I'm closer today than I was yesterday to apprehending that which I could not apprehend before and they are the plans, purposes and future God has called me to.

Chapter Ten

<u>Letting Go: New Beginning: Destiny!</u>

"For I know the thoughts that I think toward you, saith the Lord, thoughts of peace, and not of evil, to give you an expected end."
Jeremiah 29:11

Three years of discipleship and I would soon find out that God was ready to move me into the place in which I would live out my destiny. He was getting ready to shift me swiftly! However, the move didn't come as I expected it would. In fact, I was caught off guard. I didn't realize that God had actually changed the course of my life until after it was said and done. The instructions came step by step. As I obeyed one command, He would reveal another one to me. At the time, I didn't know that I would be going anywhere, where I would be going or what I would be doing. I was merely delighting in pleasing God. By this time, I had grown accustomed to hearing His voice and obeying it when there was an instruction from Him. However, I would face a crucial test of practicing my faith by stepping out in obedience to some challenging instructions from God. This is a time in my spiritual walk when God was testing me as He had done Abraham by telling him to sacrifice Isaac, his only promised son (see Genesis 22:1-19).

Within those three years, it seemed like I had been through a long season of spiritual boot camp. By now, I was at the point in my spiritual walk where one could readily see the call of ministry on me. The prophetic had pretty much been in operation since the day I got delivered, or better yet, my turning point. However, within those few years, I had really grown into and gotten comfortable with the prophetic teaching and prayer ministry which I had been called to. At the time, I hadn't thought of myself as a preacher or called to the office of ministry. After all, I was an actress pursuing a career in Hollywood, not a minister. I was just living out my passion for the things of God and benefiting from the fruit of the sacrifices I had made in the years leading up to that point.

Fruit was coming forth from what I had been sowing into my spiritual life. I stopped going to a lot of Hollywood events and hanging around certain people. My whole circle of friends changed pretty much overnight. God had chosen an inner circle of friends for me since I had rededicated my life to Him, and I must say, it was quite beneficial to have formed a sisterhood of believers who were like-minded. If we believe that iron does sharpen iron, we must also accept that evil communications do corrupt good manners. Simply because I spent most of my recreational time with these women of God, I was the more sharpened in my spiritual walk, rather than influenced by the lifestyles and mindsets of my former worldly friends.

Concerning my former friends, I didn't have to pick up the phone and tell them that I couldn't have anything more to do with them; God just drifted us apart. There were no hard feelings on either side. I've learned that in many cases, it's not that the other party is bad, it's just that sometimes, who they are is in conflict with what God wants to do in us. If we are careful not to run back and try to undo what God has done, we will have more room in our lives for people who have something to do with our purposes and destinies. God sends people to us who come on assignment, either to give us something spiritual or benefit from what we can give them spiritually. Either way, we benefit.

This was the case being on the set of a certain popular sitcom for two seasons. I sat with a group of women who worked crew with me and our job was not the only thing we had in common. Amazingly, we were all hungry Christian women as well who were equally yoked with one another. For our job assignment, we would have to be on the set for several hours during the day and there was a lot of rushing and a lot of waiting. We worked hard, but we also had a lot of time on our hands. During those down times, we would huddle together and have Bible study. This is where I could see the fruit of what I had been doing coming forth. Oftentimes, God puts us in situations where we are in conducive atmospheres when it's our seasons to birth out something spiritually. For me, the atmosphere was conducive to the birth of my teaching ministry. At the time, I didn't have a clue that this is what was taking place. As I stated before, I was just doing something I loved doing: sharing my faith and what I was learning with others as I pursued my career as an actress.

Before I knew it, we were all bringing our Bibles and looking forward to the first opportunity to gather together and break open the Word as we gathered on the set daily. Each of the ladies contributed to the studies, however, for my part, God used me to bring some powerful truth and revelation for practical application of the Word of God to our lives. At one point, one of the women said that as I talked, she had a vision that tiny little swords were spewing out of my mouth in the place of the words that I spoke. Another time, a woman told me that as I prophetically exhorted her in the Word and then prayed for her, she saw a penetrating fire in my eyes. In those times of teaching and gathering with those ladies, I could feel the intense anointing of God working with me and through me. My ministry gifts were in operation and the ministry gifts of the Holy Spirit were at work as well, so what I was doing came easy. Also, the countless hours I spent in the Word with all my study material laid out on my living room floor day after day, week after week and month after month helped. In fact, I was beginning to see a spiritual harvest in my changed lifestyle.

Everywhere I went, I went with the attitude of sharing the gospel with others. I was also operating in the ministry call of evangelism with a heavy burden and love for the lost. I was zealous to open my mouth to perfect strangers and acquaintances whenever I was prompted to do so. I had become a walking epistle, sharing the prophetic with anyone God put in my path of life; I evangelized in grocery stores, public bathrooms, and even restaurants. I remember once being in a popular soul food restaurant, sharing the gospel and the prophetic word to an old friend I had run into who was, at the time, an up and coming comedian. He has since gone on to have a great career in Hollywood.

This particular restaurant was always packed with people and the tables were very close together. He happened to be seated at a table next to where I was sitting with a few friends. We both recognized one another, so we exchanged hellos and a little small talk. Before I knew it, I was in a full-fledged dissertation on the importance of having Christ in Hollywood. The Holy Spirit is faithful; He will not lead you wrong. I was in the right place at the right time to be able to witness Christ to somebody's loved one. He was actually a backsliding Christian; he had grown up in church. We were both so engaged in the Holy Spirit that neither of us seemed to notice that when I raised my voice, onlookers were gazing and listening. Eventually, we had to have our food warmed up. I didn't care if I looked like a fruitcake to some; what was important to me (and equally rewarding) was that he received the word for his life and thanked me because he had been encouraged.

After we wrapped up our conversation, a woman who was sitting next to me at the opposite table felt compelled to speak to me. She was Holy Ghost filled. I don't remember her face, but I do remember her spirit till this day. She talked to me as if she were a very proud mother. She told me that she had been listening and observing our conversation and that she knew that I didn't know this about myself, but she saw the evangelistic call on my life. She was correct. I didn't know that at the time, but when she spoke it, my spirit bore witness to the truth. I had been in the right place at the right time for a word for my life as well. On that day, both my comedian friend and I benefited. I also found out that when God confirms through others the gifts and callings He's placed on our lives, there is a certain boldness and confidence that comes forth to operate on a deeper level.

The apostle Paul exhorted us to each use our gifts in proportion to our faith (see Romans 12:1-8). This had been a season where my entire life was a favorable atmosphere for my faith to elevate to another level. People were beginning to respond to and pull on my ministry gifts. At my church, many who knew me and had heard my prayers in the prayer ministry would stop me in the hallways or in the parking lot and ask me to pray for their serious situations. I also began to pray with another minister from the prayer ministry at his request. For a short season, he would come to my house twice weekly. The first day that he showed up, he pulled out a long list of serious prayer requests; some for himself, but mostly for others that he promised he would pray for. I was honored that he would count on me to help him pray for these people since I also had a lot of respect for his ministry. Since he was a single man and I a single woman, we kept it holy and professional. Week after week, after he arrived at my house, we would get to work and we would go into some serious warfare and pray prophetic prayers against the enemy's camp. Meanwhile, the list got smaller and smaller as he would receive testimonies of the breakthroughs or answered prayers. We made a great team. He and I actually did end up going on a few dates and spent time getting to know one another, but after awhile, and especially after the prayer request list was empty, we sort of drifted apart. Nevertheless, I appreciated the time we spent laboring in prayer for the serious needs of others; it was time well spent and the reward was priceless.

I continued to lend my gifts and time to God's people. I would receive calls from young women requesting prayer and a word almost nightly. I would hold prayer meetings in my home and overnight sleep-ins where many were blessed. Once, while I was fasting, I brought a homeless woman into my home and stayed up with her all night, giving her counsel and comfort. During the time spent listening to her, I learned that the reason she was homeless was because she was handing over her monthly social security checks to some heartless cult leader who was lying to her and others. Talk about righteous indignation! I prayed her up out of that spirit of confusion. Before long, I would see her regularly at church and eventually she began to smile again because she left the cult, got a place to stay and had her teeth fixed. I was so overjoyed for her and in awe of how awesome God is that He cares for the hurting.

And He does care for the hurting. Back on the set of the sitcom I was working on at the time, one of the women from our Bible study group had a serious family issue. She shared with me that her brother had been physically abusing his girlfriend. The abuse continued even though she had become pregnant. This time, he had gotten so angry with her that he beat her and kicked her in the stomach. She had reported to my friend that beforehand, the baby was lively, moving and kicking all the time. After this particular beating, she had not felt the baby move for three days. The young lady had no family to look to, so my friend decided that she would buy the young woman a bus ticket to leave town and move in with one of her own family members who was willing to help. She asked me to come over to pray for her before she sent her away. Of course, I wanted to pray for her, so later that evening, I found myself in my car, headed to her house and praying in the Holy Ghost on the way.

I realized that everything I was doing that had to do with the gospel was not me, but the Holy Spirit in me. It was His ministry coming forth and this was one of those times that I'm glad I knew Him. As I arrived at her house, I covered myself with holy anointing oil as I learned to do through the example of my mentors. My heart went out to this young woman as I looked at her ghastly bruises and the cuts on her face, neck and arms; her wounds looked so very painful. She was so filled with shame that she couldn't even look at me when my friend introduced us. I had no idea where to begin, but as I was contemplating, I heard the Holy Spirit instruct me to encourage her and not to worry about praying for her just yet. As I opened my mouth, the anointing of God kicked in, and for a certain length of time, beautiful, powerful and encouraging words came forth on her behalf. The benevolence of God is real; it's a power that chases away shame, humiliation, unworthiness and the like. After a while, she hadn't stopped crying, but I knew that the reasons for her tears had changed. The Holy Spirit had uplifted her spirit in such a way that she had actually lifted up her head and had begun to look at me, instead of the floor as I ministered to her.

Suddenly, the Holy Spirit instructed me to lay my hands on her belly, speak to the child and command him to live. I did just that with no hesitation, just as He had groomed me to do. After a few minutes of praying, the young woman began to giggle and then, outright laugh. Finally, she blurted out, "He's kicking; I can feel him kicking!" What a glorious moment! The baby that was once lifeless in his mother's womb was now kicking profusely. We continued to encourage her in the Word, and as I said my goodbyes on that evening, I gave her one of my favorite Bibles and a little money to help with her journey. Frankly, it didn't dawn on me until I was praising God on the way home just how big of a thing He had done for this young woman. I benefited as well; my faith was alive!

That night, as I laid myself down to sleep and prayed the Lord to keep my soul, I remembered that young woman, my friend, and her family, and I thanked God for the experience. I also remembered His amazing grace to me, after all, I had also been a victim of domestic abuse. Neither of us, that young lady nor myself had become a casualty. His amazing grace is wonderful! These were the times when I could plainly see the benefit of all the time I had spent crying out to the Lord concerning my own woes, hurts, and pains from the past. I was determined to get healed and free.

The payoff was great! On that evening, I was ministry-minded. This is who I was now. I was of the mindset to help her out of the same mess I had once been through, and not of a mindset that would have left us both a crying mess. God can do a lot with a healed heart. I'm a living witness. Just a few years earlier, I was a woman with a broken heart just trying to do the best I could do for myself with what I was working with. Deliverance of indwelling demons is one thing, getting free of the mindset which opened the door that permitted them to be there is an entirely different struggle, but it is necessary!

It was all worth it, including all the fasting and suffering I had in my flesh and the times I elected to stay home and enjoy the Word rather than go out for a night of entertainment. I enjoyed the many prayer walks, meditating on scriptures in order to hide the Word in my heart, the worship, devotion and honor that I had given to God, even when I didn't feel like it; it was all worth it. I wasn't just doing those things so that I could have a better life, even though my life is better because of those few years. Needless to say, God honored my decision to want to get free and stay free, mainly because He knew that where He was bringing me to, there would be many who would need to experience the same type of freedom I'd received. I was beginning to get it. As deep of a healing that I could encounter with God for myself is as deep as I could bring healing to another person who was suffering. During that season, every time I had the opportunity to bring hope to someone in need, I learned to appreciate the fruit of my labor and the opportunity to increase my faith.

My faith was built up strong too. I felt like I was ready to go to the next level. I was sold out to God, even though I wasn't perfect, after all, I had dealt with a lot of sin in my life. I was a new woman. And so, I thought that I would be going to the next level in my acting career. I had just been cast for a guest star role on a sitcom, booked a national commercial and my audition opportunities had actually increased. This is when God would begin to really challenge my faith and obedience. I was getting ready to go to the next level, but not how I expected.

I definitely would need my built-up faith because what I heard God tell me to do next was a test of my faith, and I couldn't give any justifiable excuse for not heeding His command. By this time, I had practiced being in His presence and hearing His voice so much that I was able to distinguish His voice from the Devil's voice and my own voice. I couldn't commence rebuking the Devil or casting it off by trying to convince myself that it was just my imagination. One day during prayer, God spoke to me and said, "I want you to leave your talent agency." When He spoke this, I understood Him to mean that He wanted me to leave acting and not just my agency. This was a monumental request since, as long as I could remember, my earnest desire in life was to go to Hollywood and become a star. It was how I identified myself; it was who I thought I was. As far as I knew, this was what I was born to do; it was my God-given destiny, or was it? When I set out to California a few years earlier, my mind was set on acting or die trying! It was all I wanted in life, but when God spoke this to me, I readily said yes in my heart, with no questions asked.

A part of me was thinking that this was like the story of Abraham when God tested him by commanding him to sacrifice Isaac, his only promised son. Abraham obeyed the

Lord's command, and when Isaac asked where the sacrifice was, Abraham responded by telling him, "My son, God will provide for himself a lamb for a burnt offering." Of course, Abraham loved his son, and more importantly, he understood that Isaac had a destiny that had not yet been fulfilled. God had promised Abraham that his seed would bless his people, the nation, and the world. Abraham knew Isaac played a role in the fulfillment of that promise. Nevertheless, Abraham knew God's voice so well that he didn't have to second-guess himself in being obedient. Instead, he simply resolved to trusting God. He understood God works in ways we don't understand all the time. His thoughts are higher than our thoughts and His ways higher than our ways (see Isaiah 55:8-9). This is what I knew to do. Trust God and resolve it in my heart that I didn't have to understand His way; I simply had to do it. Whatever He says, I will just do it.

At the end of the story, as Abraham lifted the knife to sacrifice his son, God did provide him with a burnt offering, saying the following to Abraham. Genesis 22:10-14, "And the angel of the Lord called unto him out of heaven, and said, Abraham, Abraham: and he said, Here am I. And he said, Lay not thine hand upon the lad, neither do thou any thing unto him: for now I know that thou fearest God, seeing thou hast not withheld thy son, thine only son from me. And Abraham lifted up his eyes, and looked, and behold behind him a ram caught in a thicket by his horns: and Abraham went and took the ram, and offered him up for a burnt-offering in the stead of his son. And Abraham called the name of that place Jehovah–jireh: as it is said to this day, In the mount of the Lord it shall be seen." Since Jehovah-jireh means, "the Lord will provide," I was thinking that He was telling me to leave my agency so that He would become my exclusive agent. Nowadays, I chuckle at the thought, but it is possible.

On the other hand, this command really didn't come as a big shock to me. As I took the time to digest what God was asking me to do, it made sense to me since I had begun to lose my desire for acting and the whole Hollywood scene within that past year. I thought it was just a phase I was going through since there had been such a radical change in my life, but the truth is that ministry had become the new love of my life. I still did not have a clear picture of what it was that God was calling me to; I just knew that I needed to trust Him and obey His voice. I found that just like Abraham, obeying God was easy to do.

Another reason it was not difficult to obey Him was because of everything I had been doing in those few years. God was imparting His desires in my heart. I was delighting in Him with my lifestyle and mindset; I had become a worshipper. Psalm 37:4 reads, "Delight thyself also in the Lord: and he shall give thee the desires of thine heart." According to the

Strong's Concordance, the Hebrew word used here for "delight" actually means to become soft, delicate or pliable. This means that a child of God "delights" in the Lord to allow his or her heart to become sensitive to Him, His ways and His Kingdom. While I was busy worshipping God, fasting, praying and seeking His will and doing His will, my heart became more pliable because, unbeknownst to me, He was busy imparting His desires into my heart. Proverbs 16:2-3 (AMPC) sums it up this way, "All the ways of a man are pure in his own eyes, but the Lord weighs the spirits (the thoughts and intents of the heart). Roll your works upon the Lord [commit and trust them wholly to Him; He will cause your thoughts to become agreeable to His will, and] so shall your plans be established and succeed." Had it not been for those three years, I would not have been able to digest the command to leave my agency and my acting career. The reason it was so easy for me to obey Him was that while I was delighting, He was slowly causing me to exchange my dreams for His dream and my will for His will.

I've learned that when God tells you to do something, He means for you to do it immediately or as soon as possible, plus, you probably shouldn't tell anyone what He has commanded you to do. When I shared God's instructions for me with a few of my closest friends, I opened the door for their opinions, speculations and suggestions. Thank God that at the end of the day, they encouraged me to be obedient to what I heard. Spirit-filled people who love you may not understand what God is saying to you, but they do understand that God is saying something to you. On the other hand, the people involved in your life who don't understand your relationship with God could serve as major obstacles to your obedience if you allow them.

On my way to the agency, the Spirit of the Lord warned me that when I arrived at the agency, there would be someone there who would try to get me to stay. Sure enough, one of my agent's assistants took me to the side and in a hushed tone, asked me if I had another agent already. When I told him that I did not, he proceeded to explain to me why I should stay in the agency until I signed with another agent. I kindly looked him in the eyes and said to him, "No thank you. Just give me my contract and headshots." I had a good agent; she was kind, generous and she worked hard for me, but I had to obey the Lord. If we linger too long with what God tells us to do, it will hinder Him from giving us our next set of instructions. There would be many more profound instructions coming my way.

Because I didn't linger in the first instruction, soon after I left my agent, God impressed upon my heart to leave my church home as well. Now, this was a big step for me. My home church and the circle of people and friends there were a major part of my life. The truth is that when God ask you to give up something, He has already uprooted you from it. All you need to do is be obedient and walk away. Again, when I got honest with myself, the truth was that for some time, I had been feeling distant and far removed from all that had been familiar to me. I just didn't know how to express it. So when He nudged my heart and then, showed me what church to visit, it was easy for me to obey Him. There were people who gave me a hard time when I announced that I would be leaving the church. Some of the people from the church, especially from the prayer ministry, called and even came over to my house. Some told me that they were praying that I would come back because I hadn't heard from God. Others outright accused me of having lost my salvation. Nonetheless, I held my ground and refused to be swayed by the voices of people and the Devil. This was certainly a time where I proved that I was ready to stand on my faith alone if I had to. Thank God I didn't have to because my closest friends gathered around me with support, prayer and encouragement. It was a pretty challenging time in my life. God was uprooting me from a lot in a short period of time.

In fact, He moved so quickly that shortly after I left my church, I received instructions to have a yard sale. I thought the purpose of the sale was to get rid of some of my belongings. It wasn't until after I began to plan for this weekend event that I received the understanding that I would not be selling just a few things, but I needed to get rid of a lot of things, including my furniture. People sure were looking at me with suspicion in their eyes when I told them the price on some things, including designer shoes, handbags, belts, and furniture. I pretty much gave it away; all of it. When it was all said and done, I was left with about six large moving boxes of some personal items, a few clothes, and a few small household items. By this time, my heart was fixed on Jesus; I really didn't care about stuff. I can say that I really trusted God. I knew that He would provide my every need. During the course of the weekend of the yard sale, God confirmed in my heart that I was moving and He showed me where I would be going. I would be moving across town to live with an elderly aunt. Again, all I could say was, "Yes, Lord". As I was obedient in one thing, He would reveal the next step I was to take.

I lived with my elderly aunt for several months before receiving a phone call from my sister in Florida. I had pretty much settled in at my aunt's house. We enjoyed one another's company. On most evenings, we would sit and talk and she would fill me in on the family history. She was funny too; she really knew how to tell a good story and I enjoyed her company. I know that I had been a great comfort to her as well because she would often say so. This was the reason I was so torn when the call came in from my sister. At the time, I had just finished managing a gospel stage play, plus, I was still attending a church where I didn't know anyone and I was continuing to fellowship with a few of my close friends, even though the dynamics of those relationships changed to some degree. Things were peaceful, but had pretty much come to a standstill. I was just waiting on God's instruction concerning my acting career, even though I felt removed from acting.

As I was enjoying a conversation with my sister, she invited me to come and visit her for an undetermined length of time. I hesitated and reluctantly told her that I would consider it. When I hung up, I told God that if it was His will for me to go, then show me how to get there. A sign came in the following week through a phone call from my brother. He was planning to drive to California, drop off a vehicle and fly back home. Before he purchased his airline ticket, he wanted to check with me to see if I wanted to drive my car from California to our family reunion in Michigan with him. He then said that after we left the reunion, we could go on to Florida to visit our sister. I don't know if he'd previously had a conversation with our sister or not. At this point, it didn't matter. God's answer was too obvious. I heard myself say "Yes."

Even when I left LA and arrived in Florida, I anticipated coming back to pick up where I had left off. I considered this trip a part of my journey and a much needed vacation away from the Hollywood scene. I had to ask myself a pointed question: If I was going to return to California, why was everything falling into place so nicely? I began to settle in, my sister found me a job and I found a church to attend. Honestly, at the time, I thought God planted me at that church for a season while I was there in Florida. I became a member and joined the prayer ministry. One day, while I was taking a prayer walk, I heard the Lord say to me that I was officially in ministry. He said that the ministry He had placed me in involved serving my family. So, that's what I did: I served my family. I cleaned, cooked, bought groceries when I could and helped pay bills. I also shared the gospel with anyone in the house who would loan me their ears. I was officially in the ministry of serving.

I loved being with my sister and her family. While there, she and I spent much needed time catching up and I was able to get reacquainted with my nieces, nephews and another sister who lived nearby. Eventually, they began to attend church with me. Everything wasn't perfect all the time, but all in all, it was good for me to be back around family. Back in Hollywood, I was used to living alone, having my own space and enjoying my single life. I found myself faced with another reality in life and that was my responsibility toward family relations. I have to give it to my sister and brother-in- law; they held it down. Even though their lives were pretty challenging at times, they were determined to persevere and that they did. I must say that coming out of that season of living with them gave me a new respect for them both.

After a while, I began to feel the pangs of loneliness and a yearning for my circle of friends back in Los Angeles. By this time, I had been in Florida for several months and I really hadn't heard from God since He told me that I was to serve my family. Meanwhile, I was attending a church that I still felt like a stranger in. I was really missing the wholesome Christian fellowship I had grown accustomed to back in LA. At the present church, I felt like I didn't belong and that the people there were cold towards me and my nephew who would accompany me to church every Sunday. It wasn't that the people were unfriendly; I believe that I was just out of the will of God. I simply hadn't found the church He wanted me to be a part of yet. Especially, since I was the one who chose it and not Him; that much I knew was true. Before leaving California, I had gone online and found a popular mega church to attend during my stay in Florida. I didn't pray about it. I just assumed that since it was similar to what I was used to in a church, it was what God wanted for me. When getting to Sunday morning and midweek services began to become a burden for me, I took that as a sign that I needed to seek God's wisdom on the matter. In the meantime, I just set out to visit every church in the area. Sunday after Sunday, I visited one church after the other with my nephew in tow.

I found myself becoming a little disgruntled about everything and anything. This was mainly because I didn't have a quiet place to pray and to give devotion the way that I had grown used to. I was really missing my worship songs and the long hours I once had that allowed me to soak in the presence of God. It seemed those times were gone and I was grieved. Up until this time, I had been able to steal away little quiet moments to study the Word and pray since I found myself home alone sporadically. But, for the most part, to be alone with God, I was able to take prayer walks whenever I could and I went to a local park and sat in my car. I'm glad I'd spiritually arrived at the place I was in prior to coming to Florida. Otherwise, I would have been a mess. Once again, I was able to appreciate the fruit of having made sacrifices when I had the opportunity to do so.

One day, after getting tired of the daily pity party, I finally came to my senses and realized that if I didn't change my attitude, God would do it for me. I knew that He required more from me and it was time to stop feeling sorry for myself and give Him more. I brought myself into focus again, went on a fast and continued on with my daily prayer walks. I began to encourage myself as David did when he needed it most (see I Samuel 30:6). One day, I found myself talking to God about my loneliness. This was one of those moments where I knew that this was God and not me. I hadn't really talked to Him about being married before. There was just one brief conversation that I could recall shortly before leaving LA that I had engaged in with Him. I told Him that if I never got married, that that would be okay with me. I would continue to serve Him as a single woman for the rest of my life. It was not an in-depth conversation where I would pour my heart out to Him.

But now, on this prayer walk with clear thoughts and a pure heart, I found myself sincerely seeking to be married. After He patiently listened to me pour my heart out for this cause, God responded. His words came in question form, "Have you considered my servant, Charles?" I was literally flabbergasted! First, I was not expecting such an expedient response, and secondly, Charles Turner III, as I understood it, had gotten married. Plus, I happened to know a little something about his character. He had been my prayer partner from the prayer ministry and I knew that if he had gotten married, he wouldn't have taken too kindly to me contacting him. I had briefly dated him and expressed interest at one time, so contacting him would have been an insult both to him and his wife. That would have just been rude! Besides, I didn't have his phone number anymore, and how would I look pursuing a man? Isn't it the man who finds a wife? Of course, I told God this bit of information. Yes, I proceeded to tell the facts to the all-knowing God. Needless to say, I didn't hear any response from Him anytime soon.

So, it was up to me. Either I would believe what I thought was true or act on God's last words to me. Once I made the decision to contact him, I remembered that I still had his email address. Now, I don't know if it was God-inspired or my own wit, but I had an idea. I would include his email address with a group of my friends and send out an email blast of one of those encouraging spiritual poems. In the case that he was married, no harm would be done and I wouldn't look as if I was pursuing him. Brilliant! If it was as God had said, then hopefully, he would take the bait and reach out to me. God was right, of course; He's always right. Two days later, I checked my email and, lo and behold, I had an email from my future husband. Charles's response to me expressed interest in knowing what I was doing and where I was. In fact, he later confirmed that within that week, he had asked the Lord where I was because he needed to get closure on whether or not I was his wife. When we'd briefly dated, God had given him a detailed dream which confirmed that I was his wife. We began to correspond regularly by email, getting reacquainted and eventually, I sent my phone number to him with an invitation to call me. We spent several months getting to know one another by phone, and about six months after I had arrived in Florida, he made his first trip out from California to visit me. At that point, my life in Florida seemed to be getting a little better. I was happy again. But any woman in love is a happy one.

Meanwhile, as our relationship was growing, God showed me my new church home. He reminded me that a woman I worked with had told me about a church that happened to be right around the corner from my sister's house. I had actually passed by it on a few occasions and made a mental note to visit it, but because I was new to the area, I couldn't remember where I had seen it. The woman pointed it out to me again, so I went for a visit.

On a Wednesday night, my nephew and I walked into this little church with a big heart. As we walked in, we were greeted with warm smiles and big hugs. The Pastor greeted us as well. He looked us both in our eyes as he introduced himself and then, asked each of us our names. He rounded the greeting off with a hearty welcome and a strong handshake. Now, this church and the people in it were not what I would have chosen for myself. I was used to a mega church with gospel music, but this church was a local family church with southern gospel. After Bible study had let out, my nephew stood to his feet and said to me, "I like this church; I'm coming back." Out of all the churches we had visited in those few months (and there were a lot of them), he had never commented on any of them. I looked at him and thought to myself, "Well, if he's coming back, I'm coming back too since I would have to bring him." That following Sunday, as we walked through the doors, the pastor was there to greet us each with a hearty handshake, but what really sealed the deal for me was that he recited both of our names perfectly. That church and its members were so full of love; I knew it was home. Shortly after finding it, God reminded me of a prayer that I had prayed to Him before leaving LA. I asked Him if He would send me to a church where the ministry could use my ministry gifts at the level that I was at so that I could put them to use, after all, I wanted to continue to grow in them. Soon after joining the church, my pastor and his lovely wife did recognize the call of ministry on my life and they took me under their wings and began to pour into me. My life was rounding out again and I was beginning to think of Florida as my new home.

Meanwhile, Charles and I had gotten engaged and God told me that I would not be returning to California, but that my husband would be moving to Florida because the Lord had determined that Florida was our wealthy place. When He told me this, I responded by saying, "Okay, but you'll have to tell him that." Charles was born and raised in California. It was his home and he had never thought about or had a desire to leave it. Sure enough, in our next phone conversation, Charles confirmed that he would be moving to Florida. Things happened quickly from that point. Florida would indeed be our wealthy place. Directly following service on one Sunday morning, Charles Turner, III and I, Marilyn Love, walked down the aisle of our little family church, stood before our pastor, and with the congregation as witnesses, commenced the ceremony of marriage.

Just one year after having stepped out on faith, leaving California and all of my dreams behind, God gave me a new beginning and a new "turning point." The number eight is the number God uses to express new beginnings. We were married in the eighth month on the eighth day and we moved into a house with the address of... you guessed it: eight. We were ready for our destiny. Shortly after our marriage, we were set forth as lay-ministers by our pastors. They nurtured and trained us for pastoral ministry. We are both so grateful for the love and support they showed this newlywed couple. After one year, we were honored to become licensed and ordained ministers. To this day, I cherish the opportunity to have experienced becoming ordained and anointed for ministry alongside my husband. It was one of the dearest moments of my life. Just four years after hearing God's voice commanding me to leave my pursuit of a career in Hollywood, God gave me a new career. My husband and I were officially set forth in pastoral ministry in our own church. Surely, God had brought us into our wealthy place and I'm sure glad I chose to do it His way.

Chapter Eleven

<u>The Abundant Life: 100%: Living Out Loud!</u>

"The thief cometh not, but for to steal, and to kill, and to destroy: I am come that they might have life, and that they might have it more abundantly."
John 10:10

S ince that chance meeting in my living room with my
friend, Cyndi, when I was delivered of those demons
(the day of my "turning point"), I have not been the same. In
the three years following that day, I began to learn the life
discipline of worshipping God and practicing forgiveness as
a lifestyle. I made a commitment to become a true follower of
Jesus through discipleship. I grew in the grace of God and
acquired more knowledge of my Lord and Savior, Jesus
Christ. I fell in love with the Holy Spirit and learned to follow
His lead in life. I learned to study the Word and to hold
myself accountable to what I was learning through
wholesome Christian fellowship and mentorship. I developed
the life discipline of prayer, church attendance, tithing, giving
to God's work and serving others with my ministry gifts. The
benefits have been insurmountable.

In His presence, I found passion for living and passion for
others. I discovered my true purpose on earth, realizing that
I'm not a mistake. I obtained the revelation needed to
understand my destiny and the call of God on my life. From
that glorious day on my living room couch to this point, I
have come full circle to my "turning point." In turn, I am able
to unselfishly give my time, love and support to others in
need, helping them to experience their own "turning points."

I am free of the burdens of guilt, shame, unworthiness and
the list goes on. As a result of my own personal experience
of deliverance and emotional healing, I'm able to lead others

to the way of freedom. God has counted the countless
fasting, watching, praying, my time spent in the Word, my
consistent tithes and alms and all the things I did and
experienced in those first three years as faithful. And He has
rewarded me with peace and a happy life. I'm reminded that
He affirms the true call on my life when I see the beautiful
people of God and the flourishing ministry He has given my
husband, Apostle Charles Turner III and myself, to steward
over. When I sit back and think about all God has done since
that crucial day: all the benefits and rewards, happiness and
peace, I can honestly say that the only thing I did was make
a decision to want more; He did the rest. I no longer despise
my humble beginnings because God has caused me to
triumph! It was His predestined plan for me to be called
"more than a conqueror."

Personally, I want to continue to be known as "more than a
conqueror through Christ Jesus," but how about you? Where
do you stand in life? I would not have been able to achieve
this title had I not made a decision to move past my first day
of salvation to go deeper in God. Next, I decided that I
wanted to be healed from my past and then, I got up and did
something about it. Christ can do a lot with our willingness
because there is nothing impossible with God. No matter
where you stand in life, no matter where you have come
from or what you have been through, God is able to set you
free.

Do you know that you have a purpose and destiny here on earth? Do you know what they are? God wants to reveal His plan for your life to you. He's just waiting on you to seek Him. The first step to God's wisdom for your life is in salvation. Jesus said that no man can come to the Father except by Him (John 14:6). If you have not accepted Jesus Christ into your life and you want to, just sincerely repeat the prayer at the end of this book. After that, you will be saved and can enjoy a growing relationship with God. Congratulations, if you already have a relationship with Jesus. Our salvation in Christ offers so much more than most Christians realize. I encourage you to go deeper and become "more than a conqueror" so that you can help others to conqueror.

After salvation, the first step to becoming "more than a conqueror" is that we must first conquer our old selves, who we were before Christ. If you have come from a victimized past where perhaps there was abuse, degradation or disadvantages, chances are, you may need emotional healing from your past. Healthy thinking comes only after we have conquered the "woe is me" syndrome. It's so easy to fall into a cycle of using our disadvantages in life as a crutch or an excuse to not get into life and fight the devil for the right to have success. It's called fighting the good fight of faith!

Some like to share with others about what they have been through regarding sexual abuse, drug abuse, mistreatment or having lived a degraded life in some way because they want empathy and sympathy. Christ became the ultimate victim so that no one has to stay a victim. As in the story of Joseph, God wants to use what your enemies meant for your harm for your good and for the good of others (see Genesis 50:19-21).

He can use your testimony of having become more than a conqueror. Millions of little girls and little boys across this nation are being abused, raped, mistreated, abandoned and destroyed by the enemy of our souls every day. God wants to use the pain and suffering of our lives to motivate us to help others who are in danger of going contrary to His will because of their present circumstances in life, but we must be healed before He can use us. So many of us miss out on the opportunity to fulfill our calls in life because we refuse to be healed from our pasts. To achieve the plans of God set before us, we must be whole in God, drama free and free of our own false burdens. I call them false because anything the enemy tries to give us is false.

I remember when I was just setting out in my walk with Christ. The Holy Spirit led me to the prayer ministry of our church where I would attend every weekday from 6:00 am-8:00 am. After a while of attending on a regular basis, the elder in charge of this ministry added me to the list of a small group of ministers in training. He assigned to each minister a certain day out of the month to minister the Word for twenty minutes. After a while, as he heard my testimony of having recovered from drug and alcohol addiction, he invited me to join him and another woman with the same testimony to a transitional house. This house was filled with broken women who were battling addiction, women who were transitioning from jail back to their homes. I looked forward to the time we spent every Thursday morning, directly after prayer service, ministering to these women. I felt that this was what I was born to do and I loved it.

On one particular Thursday morning, as I was driving to the transitional home, I had an emotional meltdown. At the time, there were some serious issues in my life that were causing me to feel anguish. I had been praying about them and battling through them. I thought I had it all together. On my way to the house to minister, out of nowhere, I just began to cry uncontrollably and the "woe is me" syndrome set in pretty badly. My attitude was bad on that day, so I reasoned within myself that I was just going to turn my car around and go home. I would just figure out an excuse to give later as to why I didn't show up.

I began to complain to God using phrases like, "Why me, Lord? Why does everything have to happen to me? No one cares about me, Lord! This isn't fair, Lord; that person did me wrong and now I'm suffering! Just fix it, please!" I probably added a "please" just so I could justify calling that rant a prayer. It was pretty pitiful. I had made a few bad decisions and gone into a partnership with someone from my past, even after being warned not to do it. The fact is I knew better, however, I thought this venture was retribution for my disadvantaged past. The aftermath was devastating and at that moment, I was unwilling to live out the consequences. We can call this a funny little moment or a cute meltdown, but that would be a lie. In fact, it was a self-centered, pride-filled moment that seriously needed to be addressed. A sense of entitlement had risen up and I had an attitude that implied that everything should go my way, even after I've done wrong because God owed me that much. After all, I have been through a lot in my life, so in my mind, I thought I should get a pass. I was a mess. That's how a woman who gives herself permission to live as a victim carries on.

Of course, I got myself together and repented after that rant, but this didn't happen until after I had heard from the Lord. In the middle of my tantrum, that loving, small and still voice spoke to me and said, "Daughter, how can you minister to others when you carry so much of a burden?" Notice that He didn't address my prayer request; instead, He pointed out my responsibility to others as a woman of God with a call on her life. And if I wasn't willing to go through this suffering in order to be transformed in my mind, I would eventually sabotage the opportunity to fulfill my purpose and destiny in life. He continued by saying, "Get over yourself and trust Me that I'm working in your life to reconcile your bad choices." That was hard, but it was true. God wanted me to continue focusing on what He had set in my path to do at the time and that was serving the women who were in need.

It was necessary for my character to change and my thinking patterns to come into alignment with His perspective and not my past. A perfect setting for my therapy was ministering at this transitional home week after week where the women had similar backgrounds as mine.

As I studied the Word and taught it, I was the first to receive it and then, the first to face the choice to either submit to it or not. Looking back at that day, what amazes me the most is how my attitude towards doing something that I absolutely loved to do for God changed so drastically within the blink of an eye. That day, I was reminded of how imperative it is to get healed from my past. That was a season where I came face to face with a lot of hard realities about myself. I was determined to change, and through much fasting, praying and just plain ole perseverance, I was able to overcome. Part of overcoming is coming to a place where we can share our personal stories in a way that is productive and glorify God, rather than the Devil.

We can not help others out of the cage of misery if we are not willing to do what is necessary in order to escape it ourselves. A person with a victim's mentality is in danger of being exploited. Sometimes, when we have been through hardships and have not done anything to escape the emotional devastation of our pasts, we put ourselves at risk of becoming our own worst enemy. We become the culprits of our own exploitation by telling the story of our griefs and sorrows with the wrong motives and intent. This only reinforces the victim mentality in others who need to be delivered. It's called the blind leading the blind into a ditch. We are called to be the light for someone's darkness.

Those with victim mentalities continually glorify the Devil's work. Through their words or deeds, they give others permission to continue to label them as victims. Instead of the message of the gospel, they send the message of bondage by demonstrating the belief that it's okay for others to wallow in their woes when they have good excuses.

I'm careful not to minimize anyone's pain and suffering, but there comes a time in our lives that we must choose to pick up our bed and walk. When we are born again, we are also given God's grace to help in our times of need. When grace comes, there's no longer an excuse for us not to be made well, regardless of the circumstance or how long one has been in a certain position or ailment. We have to make the decision to stop putting our expectations and burdens on people. We should, instead, look to Jesus who has promised that all can be healed. We can't afford to sit around and wait for people to give us what we want and need on a silver platter, especially in this day. It's good to accept a little help now and then, but God wants us to be givers and not takers in this world. And He has given us the help we need to do so. We can make a decision to get up and then, God meets us there with His beautiful gift of grace so that we can help ourselves.

In John 5:1-8, Christ came to a man in Jerusalem who was in great need of healing. This man laid by the pool Bethesda. It had five porches; five is the number for grace. Sick people, blind people, lame people and others with all sorts of ailments lay by this pool waiting for the moving of the water. Ever so often, an angel would step down into the pool and stir the water. We know that the grace that is offered through salvation is for us all. "Come… whosoever will, let him take the water of life freely" (see Revelations 22:17). However, the grace at this pool was different. Only one person could experience it at a time. The one healed had to have been the one stepping into the water immediately after the angel stirred it. The first people to get in were healed of their diseases, infirmities or whatever they were ailed by. Jesus knew this certain man lying by the pool had an infirmity that he'd suffered with for thirty-eight years. He said to the man, "Do you want to be made well?" The sick man answered Him, "Sir I have no man to put me into the pool when the water is stirred up; but while I am coming, another steps down before me." Jesus said to him, "Rise, take up your bed and walk." And immediately the man was made well, took up his bed, and walked (see John 5:1-8).

In this story, Jesus came to a man who was in great need because of a condition he had been suffering with for thirty-eight long years. He asked him a simple question, "Do you want to be made well?" Of course, he wanted to be healed; he had been there for quite some time already, waiting and hoping that the day would come when someone would help him get into the stirring water. Every time that water stirred and someone climbed in before him was a missed opportunity for him to recover. He had a lot of missed opportunities, since he had been there awhile. The man gave a reasonable excuse as to why he was still lame after having spent a great deal of his time at the pool, "Sir I have no man to put me into the pool." That was the truth and his reality was that he indeed needed help. He was lame; he could not help himself. Lying there and waiting for someone to help him get into the water immediately after it was stirred had to be a difficult situation for him. It's obvious that he had no one who cared enough to help him get well. His hope was misplaced if his healing depended on someone else coming along and lifting him up.

I imagine at that pool, the mentality was, "Only the fittest survive" and "Every man for himself." That may have been the case then, but Jesus showed up and the playing field was evened out. After all, wherever Jesus shows up, grace shows up and grace gives everyone the same opportunity to be partakers of it if they so choose. Jesus didn't wait for the man's answer to His question; He simply gave him a command, "Rise, take up your bed and walk." The Bible tells us that the lame man did just that. "And immediately the man was made well, took up his bed, and walked" (John 5:9). First, the man was "made well", and then he "took up his bed." After that, he "walked" out of his lameness. Oftentimes, I wonder what would have happened if this man, after being made well, chose not to pick up his bed. The answer is always the same: he would not have been able to walk and he would have missed another opportunity to be made whole.

When grace comes, it's always on the individual whether they will take advantage of it or not. Healing and deliverance are a part of our salvation's package. Consider Psalm 103:3-4. It tells us about the forgiving nature of God. "Who forgiveth all thine iniquities; who healeth all thy diseases; Who redeemeth thy life from destruction; who crowneth thee with lovingkindness and tender mercies." This promise means that when we get saved, we are forgiven of what caused sickness in the first place: sin! Salvation makes us candidates of the healing power of God.

There comes a time when we are confronted with the option of healing and deliverance from our pasts. It begins with the gospel, but then, it's our responsibility to make that next decision. Healing is the kingdom children's bread. Jesus said, "It isn't right to take food from the children and throw it to the dogs" (see Matthew 15:26). Do we want to be whole or are we willing to settle for the dog's portion? Sadly, many who have come from troubled pasts in the body of Christ never make it past salvation at the altar. Some come to Jesus and get sincerely saved, and after that, they take a seat in a pew and fall asleep. It is as if they are hiding from the abundant life that Jesus promised them.

They end up staying the same with the same mindset, same character flaws, soul ties, regrets, grief, sorrows and disappointments, not realizing that these are the very things that can halt their spiritual growth and progress in life. Many of us relive our past lives of abuse and mistreatment, and because of this, we constantly come into contact with the same type of people who the enemy used to victimize us in the first place. This had been my case, but thank God I finally read the memo of grace. Albert Einstein said that insanity is doing the same thing over and over again while expecting different results!

Insanity has to do with one's mindset! The negative patterns of thinking that kept me in bondage to the victim's mentality and failure were finally abolished! I'm glad that when the opportunity came knocking at my door yet again, I finally decided to let Him come in and stay this time. I'm glad that my knowledge of the benefits of salvation didn't end there either.

I said yes to God when He offered me a healing and deliverance program that He tailor made just for me. Because I said yes, the cycle of unholy soul ties was utterly destroyed and I can live in freedom from the pain of rejection, abandonment, guilt, shame, condemnation and unworthiness. With God's help, I was able to break strongholds, proclivities, and cycles of fear and failure in my life. It wasn't easy and it didn't happen overnight, but thanks be to God, which giveth us the victory through our Lord Jesus Christ that at this time in my life, I'm walking strong in the Lord and in the power of His might, while wearing the full armor of God (see Ephesians 6:10-17). I am now living an abundant life.

Christ has promised us an abundant life and I'm determined to live it out to its fullest. Living the abundant life has little to do with how much stuff we can acquire in our lifetime. It's nice to have a nice home, a car that you own, a wardrobe in your closet that you can be proud to wear and food on your table. I'm grateful for all these things for myself and my loved ones. However, Christ taught us in the fifth chapter of Matthew, that we don't have to be so concerned with those things. As long as we are seeking God, His kingdom and the right things to do, those things, which are God's will for our lives, will be added to us.

For me, living the abundant life speaks to the fact that I've become willing to pick up my cross and carry it. The cross we bear in life are the things that God uses to refine our character and faults; it's the outward pressure that helps change the inner man. I learned that indeed, God delights to give us the kingdom, however, He wants us to be faithful servants fit to steward over what He releases to us. When I am willing to endure the sufferings of this life, I have given myself the opportunity to change the flaws and character faults that hinder my progress in life.

Think about the man at the pool of Bethesda who was healed from being lame. That bed he laid on in his sickness could have represented his cross in life. In his sickness, it only served as the thing that kept him comfortable as he laid on it year after year, lame. When he was made well, he was able to pick it up and walk towards doing things for himself, and eventually, helping others in life. It became a part of his testimony. I imagine that every time he looked at it, he was thinking of the great future and possibilities ahead of him because he had been made well; he didn't focus so much on his past ailment. Because he was healed, he could help himself and eventually, help others in need. In Galatians 6:2, we are told to "Bear ye one another's burdens, and so fulfil the law of Christ." Our salvation gets us into heaven, but what we do on earth with it, earns us rewards in heaven. He has given us the ministry of reconciliation. We are to be in the right frame of mind and right spiritual condition to help others find their way to Christ in their time of need.

Whatever my lot may be in life, that cross is the will of the Father. That cross represents my commitment to live life God's way. I no longer want to find ways to get out of bearing my own cross. Whatever trouble or afflictions I need to go through, it's just the cross I have to bear. In fact, I want to get so good at carrying my cross that I'm able to multi-task. I want to carry my cross while helping someone else to bear their cross in their time of need.

When I look at my cross, I'm reminded that I've died with Christ and He lives through me in this world; my life is not my own. My cross keeps me humbled and submitted to God. I've made the commitment to sacrifice my will for God's will. The cross trains me to keep my emotions and my way of thinking in check. When I'm going through a rough time and when things get hard and I can't see the road ahead, my cross is there to remind me that whatever I'm going through or whatever pain I have to suffer is for my good, the good of others and for God's glory. It reminds me that I should count it all joy to suffer for Christ's sake knowing that the patience I acquire from the storm will help me to be a better servant and to enjoy a brighter future.

The cross keeps my faith alive, knowing I can do all things through Christ who strengthens me. The cross reminds me that just like the man at the pool, no matter how long I have suffered, life always gets better. I shouldn't give up on the plan of God for my life just because of a storm. When the storms come, I get upon that cross and die to self, self-will, selfish thoughts, fear or whatever is in me that would hinder my progress on the road to destiny. I have to stay on the narrow road that leads to eternal life, where my ultimate destiny lies.

Abundant living is not about getting material stuff; all that is good! Paul said that he doesn't regard need because he learned to be content in whatever situation he found himself in (see Philippians 4:11). The abundant life is about finding happiness. Contentment is ease. Regardless of where we find ourselves in our lives, we can have peace of mind. It's not that we settle for less and continue to live middle-of-the-road lives. Of course, we want to strive for the very best life we can possibly have on earth, however, any life worth living does not come easy. On the way to success, purpose, and ultimate destiny, we are going to face hardships and sufferings. Contentment in whatever comes our way helps us to stay calm through that storm so that we can continue to progress toward the mark of the high calling of God, doing it His way.

Paul continued to explain contentment in Philippians 4:12-13, "I know both how to be abased, and I know how to abound: every where and in all things I am instructed both to be full and to be hungry, both to abound and to suffer need. I can do all things through Christ which strengtheneth me." Paul was admitting that in spite of all the victories and many achievements in Christ he had gotten, there had also been times in his walk with Christ that he had been humiliated, crushed and demeaned.

This was the man who met many perils in his life for the sake of the gospel, but it was a part of the plan of God to fulfill his call in life. He was beaten with rods, and not once or twice, but three times. He was stoned and left for dead, plus, he had been in three different shipwrecks. In one of those wrecks, he spent a full night and day in the sea hanging on for his life. He had been robbed and rejected by his own countrymen. He'd found himself in dangerous cities, in the wilderness, at sea and among false brethren. He suffered in the cold, being hungry, thirsty, and naked. Yet, having gone through all these perils, Paul was still alive and thriving in Christ, determined to live life on God's terms and not his own. Through all his sufferings and successes, Paul learned that no matter what life throws at him, he could do all things through Christ who was the source of his strength.

We can not afford to stay stuck in our old ways and our old thinking patterns. If we remained stuck, we would continue to live our lives the way Satan wants us to live them until we reach heaven. Jesus came to give us life and that more abundantly! Wherever we find ourselves in life, whatever positions or circumstances we have to face, whatever afflictions must come because of those circumstances, whatever the case may be, we understand that we too can do all things through the strength of Christ. This is living the abundant life!

If I can be truthful about a portion of my childhood, let me share this with you: I knew that I was loved, and there were many who made sacrifices for me while bearing their own crosses. However, at times, I felt that I was a mistake. Not only did I feel like I was a mistake, there were times when I was treated as if I were a mistake. Furthermore, I learned from my own perceptions how to treat myself as a mistake. But I have since learned that there are no mistakes in God! I've learned how to embrace my beginnings because the scars of my past are the marks I bear to remind me that I made it out.

I took the time to identify those issues of my past. I stared them in the face, got completely honest with myself and called each issue what it really was. I came to terms with whatever it might have cost me to have gone through each crisis. I stepped out in faith, and with the love of God, forgave all parties involved... even myself. I wiped the slate clean and now, they owe me nothing. I understand now that people do what they know to do, most people do the best they can do in life and you can never truly understand every situation. I decided to live life in freedom from bitterness, disappointments and regrets. It became my personal declaration! In doing so, I was able to rise above every dark circumstance from my past, not allowing them to haunt me time after time as they did so often, stealing my joy in life. I realized that if I didn't get free, my birthright, my happiness and my power would continue to be dictated by my past hurts, sorrows and the Devil.

I chose to overcome and take authority and responsibility for my own life and where I stand as a woman of God. I've decided to spend the rest of my life "living out loud," taking 100% responsibility for the choices I make in life, finding my own joy in Christ and holding no grudges toward those who chose to misuse and persecute me. I've decided that I'm just going to keep following Jesus and keep my eyes fixed on him. Wherever He leads me is good enough for me.

I've stopped living life on my own terms and have picked up my cross, understanding that the cross we have to bear in life is the very thing that can keep us moving in the right direction. When we see Jesus carrying His cross, He's carrying it towards that ultimate thing He came to earth to do and that is to fulfill His destiny. It was God's plan and will for His life; it was His purpose. In His earthly ministry, Jesus fulfilled His mission here on the earth.

Through keeping Jesus's example, we too can fulfill our God ordained destinies in life, for the promises are sure in Him!

Jeremiah 29:11 declares, "For I know the thoughts that I think toward you, says the Lord, thoughts of peace and not of evil, to give you a future and a hope." I'm a daughter of the Most High God. Surely, I have a future, a hope and a destiny! I'm proving it everyday because I'm determined to LIVE OUT LOUD!

END

Prayer for Salvation

God loves you and counts your life as something valuable. John 3:16 says, "For God so loved the world that He gave His only begotten Son, that whoever believes in Him should not perish but have everlasting life." He wants you to live the abundant life that He provided through His Son, Jesus Christ. Jesus said in John 10:10, "The thief does not come except to steal, and to kill, and to destroy. I have come that they may have life, and that they may have it more abundantly."

Sin separates man from God. Through Jesus, we can be restored to a close intimate relationship with God, allowing us to experience the abundant life Jesus promised. We must take the following four steps in order to become born again.

You must recognize the need for salvation. Romans 3:23 tells us, "For all have sinned and fall short of the glory of God" And Romans 6:23 teaches us the consequences of sin. It reads, "For the wages of sin is death, but the gift of God is eternal life in Christ Jesus our Lord."

You must recognize the solution to sin. Romans 5:8, declares, "But God demonstrates His own love toward us, in that while we were still sinners, Christ died for us." John 14:6 records Jesus's words, "Jesus said to him, "I am the way, the truth, and the life. No one comes to the Father except through Me."

You must recognize what the gospel is and believe. I Corinthians 15:3-4 explains, "For I delivered to you first of all that which I also received: that Christ died for our sins according to the Scriptures, and that He was buried, and that He rose again the third day according to the Scriptures."

You must recognize how to get the solution. Romans 10:9-10 gives us these instructions, "That if you confess with your mouth the Lord Jesus and believe in your heart that God has raised Him from the dead, you will be saved. For with the heart one believes unto righteousness, and with the mouth confession is made unto salvation."

If you desire to receive Jesus Christ in your heart, simply repeat the following prayer out loud with a sincere heart. Dear God in heaven. I am a sinner. I ask You to forgive me of all sin. I ask that Jesus Christ come into my heart. According to I Corinthians 15:3-4, I believe the gospel. I confess with my mouth that Jesus Christ is Lord and I believe in my heart that He rose from the dead on the third day. Thank you, Jesus, for coming into my heart and saving me. Satan, you are no longer my father or lord. Jesus Christ is now Lord of my life and my new Father is YAHWEH. I ask these things in Jesus's name. Amen.

About the Author

Marilyn Turner is a Pastor of New Hope Int'l Ministries, which she and her husband, Senior Pastor, Apostle Charles Turner III co-established in 2012. Her multi-faceted prophetic and teacher's ministry is marked by deliverance, miracles, and sound Biblical preaching. She is an author, playwright, conference speaker and a Prophetess called to the nations.

Her heart is in outreach ministry, for people who are hurting. Her passion is pursuing those who are without Christ and lost. She's an active, servant and leader who runs to the battlefield first on behalf of God's people. She comes armed with warfare prayers, the belt of righteousness and the gospel of peace. Her journey to the pulpit has led her from a small town in Michigan to the bright lights of Hollywood and then to ministry.

This self-titled "country girl" has been through more than her humble smile portrays. She is one of several siblings thrown into crisis after her parents' separation and her mother's tragic illness. Her testimony is lined with abandonment, emotional abuse, physical abuse, sexual abuse and alcohol and drug addiction. Nevertheless, what did not kill her body could not kill her spirit.

This is why Marilyn is sincere in her approach to people with addictions and longstanding problems. This is also why she and her husband have the right balance of patience and compassion to carry out the Lord's vision for their growing church: New Hope Int'l Ministries. Their motto is: *Christ did not come to condemn the world and neither do we! Whosoever will, let him come.*

Marilyn is the founder of Women of Warfare Ministries, a ministry provoking women and teens to stand up for righteous living. The news about the growth and progress of this ministry has brought women from neighboring churches and communities to participate in events at N.H.I.M. After arriving, they have been delivered from sicknesses, depression, oppression and more. The fire of her anointing is spreading and unquenchable.

She is the founder of the non-profit organization, Esther's Closet. Esther's Closet is a boutique-style thrift store with a mission to clothe those in need and to offer "clothes fit for royalty at thrift store prices" in the community.

The Turners are charged with the task of reaching the harvest through dynamic preaching, teaching, prayer, praise, and worship, and they have done this faithfully for the last ten years.

In that span of time, Apostle Charles and Marilyn Turner have tirelessly evangelized, cast out devils, laid hands on the sick, won souls to the Lord and have grown the work of the kingdom at the N.H.I.M. Worship Center. They provoke the saints to righteous, victorious living and godly maturity. Believers are encouraged to study their Bibles, and to fast and pray fervently.

Prophetess Marilyn Turner's ministry is an immeasurable blessing to New Hope Int'l Ministries, the community, and to the Body of Christ worldwide.

For more information or booking, call:
954-906-2078

Or visit us at:
www.livingnhim4life.org
www.livingoutloudonpurpose.org

Made in the USA
Charleston, SC
05 May 2016